Reading ADVENTURES

3

Carmella Lieske • Scott Menking

NATIONAL GEOGRAPHIC LEARNING

CENGAGE Learning·

Australia • Brazil • Japan • Korea • Mexico • Singapore • Spain • United Kingdom • United States

Reading Adventures 3
Carmella Lieske and Scott Menking

Publisher: Andrew Robinson

Executive Editor: Sean Bermingham

Senior Development Editor: Derek Mackrell

Associate Development Editor: Claire Tan

National Geographic Editorial Coordinator:
  Leila Hishmeh

Director of Global Marketing: Ian Martin

Product Marketing Manager: Anders Bylund

Senior Content Project Manager: Tan Jin Hock

Manufacturing Planner: Mary Beth Hennebury

Compositor: Page 2, LLC.

Cover/Text Designer: Page 2, LLC.

Cover Photo: Beverly Joubert/
  National Geographic Image Collection

Acknowledgments
The Authors and Publishers would like to thank
the following teaching professionals for their
valuable feedback during the development of
this series.

Lewis Berksdale, Kanazawa Institute of
Technology, Japan; **Clare Chun**, Language
World, Korea; **John Dennis**, Hokuriku
University, Japan; **Kátia Falcomer**, Casa Thomas
Jefferson, Brazil; **Alexandra Ruth Favini**,
Escuela Graduada "Joaquin V. Gonzalez,"
Argentina; **Yuka Iijima**, Dokkyo University,
Japan; **Pia Isabella**, Colegio Nacional "Rafael
Hernández" UNLP, Argentina; **Minkyoung Koo**,
Woongin Plus Language School, Korea;
Alison Larkin, Box Hill College, Kuwait;
Laura MacGregor, Gakushuin University,
Japan; **Jill Pagels**, KAUST Schools, Saudi Arabia;
Hyunji Park, Kyunghee University, Korea;
Stephen P. van Vlack, Sookmyung Women's
University, Korea; **Deborah Wilson**, American
University of Sharjah, United Arab Emirates

For permission to use material from this text or product,
submit all requests online at **cengage.com/permissions**
Further permissions questions can be emailed to
permissionrequest@cengage.com

Library of Congress Control Number: 2012939554

ISBN-13: 978-0-8400-3039-9

ISBN-10: 0-8400-3039-8

National Geographic Learning
20 Channel Center Street
Boston, MA 02210
USA

Cengage Learning is a leading provider of customized learning solutions with
office locations around the globe, including Singapore, the United Kingdom,
Australia, Mexico, Brazil, and Japan. Locate your local office at:
international.cengage.com/region

Cengage Learning products are represented in Canada by Nelson Education, Ltd.

Visit National Geographic Learning online at **ngl.cengage.com**

Visit our corporate website at **www.cengage.com**

Printed in the United States
1 2 3 4 5 6 7 — 16 15 14 13 12

Contents

Get Ready for an Adventure!

The ruins of a village can tell us a lot about the Haida people who lived there. What can we learn? **p. 58**

Scientists found an amazing discovery at the bottom of the sea. What was it? **p. 43**

NORTH AMERICA

Amanda Kitts lost her arm in an accident. How did doctors help her? **p. 23**

In 1962, President Kennedy gave a very important speech. What was it about? **p. 69**

These thorn bugs use a special trick to frighten predators. What is it? **p. 13**

SOUTH AMERICA

Yossi Ghinsberg spent three weeks lost and alone in the rain forests of Bolivia. How did he survive? **p. 49**

What was it like to be left alone on a small boat in a huge storm? Nick Ward describes his experience. **p. 52**

At Newgrange, something amazing happens only one morning a year. What is it? **p. 84**

Hiroshi Ishiguro has a very special "twin." What is unusual about him? **p. 27**

EUROPE

Who is Charles Lutwidge Dodgson, and why is he famous? **p. 91**

ASIA

Why is Mesopotamia sometimes called "The Birthplace of Writing"? **p. 82**

In what way is modern Chinese writing similar to the writing of the ancient Mayans? **p. 75**

AFRICA

The Hadza people have very few possessions, and don't celebrate birthdays. Are they happy? **p. 105**

This woman speaks Koro. Why is this language interesting for linguists? **p. 101**

AUSTRALIA

Stromatolites are some of the oldest living things on Earth. How old are they? **p. 39**

Scope and Sequence

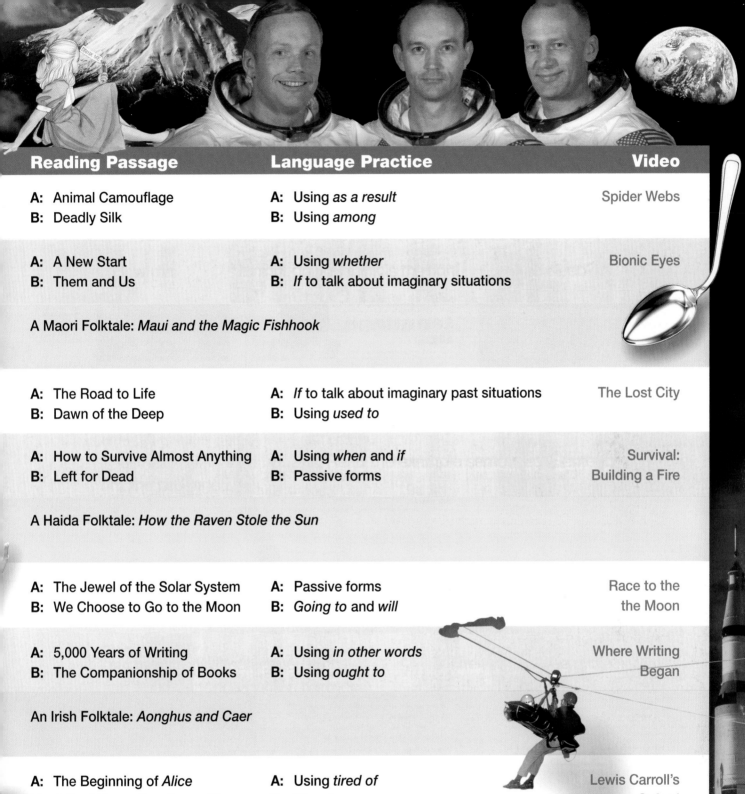

Unit Walkthrough

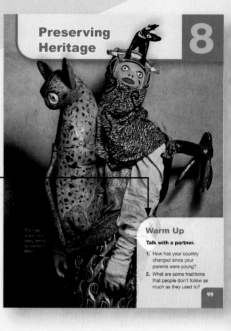

Preserving Heritage — 8

Warm Up
discussion questions introduce the unit topic.

Warm Up

Talk with a partner.

1. How has your country changed since your parents were young?
2. What are some traditions that people don't follow as much as they used to?

99

Before You Read tasks encourage students to think about the ideas in the reading.

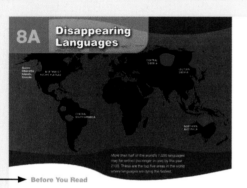

8A **Disappearing Languages**

More than half of the world's 7,000 languages may be extinct by the year 2100. These are the top five areas in the world where languages are dying the fastest.

Before You Read

A **Discussion.** Look at the map above. Do you live near any of the areas where languages are dying? What kinds of people do you think speak these languages? Talk about your ideas with a partner.

B **Definitions.** Match the words with their meanings.

| 1. allow | 2. amount | 3. economic | 4. express (v.) |
| 5. local | 6. reflect | 7. respond | 8. specific |

___ a. to show what you think or feel
___ b. to let something happen
___ c. to think carefully about something
___ d. referring to a particular thing
___ e. how much of something there is
___ f. to reply
___ g. about or related to a particular area
___ h. related to the money and businesses of a country or society

100 Unit 8 Preserving Heritage

Reading

Strategy: Predicting. What are some reasons why a language becomes endangered? Discuss with a partner. Read the passage to check your predictions.

Language Death

Every 14 days, another language dies. There are many reasons for this. Some people think more common languages have more **economic** power. Because of this, young people choose to learn a common language as they think it is more useful. Another reason is that some languages aren't written down. Guujaaw is a leader of the Haida Nation. His people have lived on the Queen Charlotte Islands, Canada, for more than 10,000 years. Their language is endangered. Traditionally, it wasn't written down, and, as a result, some people are worried that it will die one day. Guujaaw **responds** to this, "We talk to each other, listen, visit, and **trust** the spoken word. **Expressing** yourself without writing is natural." However, if Guujaaw's language and others like it are going to survive, writing may have to become part of their lives.

Too Important to Lose

When a language dies, an amazing **amount** of knowledge dies with it. To begin with, language is a huge part of the culture of the people who speak it. Language **allows** speakers to say **specific** things: words that describe a cultural idea may not translate exactly into another language. Furthermore, many endangered languages have rich spoken cultures. Stories, songs, and histories are passed on from older people to younger generations. Anthropologist Elizabeth Lindsey emphasizes this. "When an elder dies, a library is burned," she claims.

Language death also affects our knowledge about nature. Native tribes often have a deep understanding of **local** plants, animals, and ecosystems. David Harrison, an expert on endangered languages, **reflects**. "Eighty percent of [plant and animal] species have been undiscovered by science. But that doesn't mean they're unknown to humans."

Still Hope

Many languages are endangered. However, it's not too late. Children often grow up speaking two languages. "No one . . . becomes richer by abandoning . . . one language to learn another," Harrison said. If children feel both languages are important, they will use both. Therefore, it is necessary that children realize how useful their local language is.

▲ Abamu Degio speaks Koro, an Indian language with about 800 native speakers. Linguists first learned about it in 2008.

▲ Guujaaw, leader of the Haida Nation

Reading Passages are adapted and graded from authentic sources.

8A Disappearing Languages 101

Reading Comprehension

A Circle the correct answer.

Vocabulary 1. In line 9, the word **trust** means ____.
a. remember   b. believe in   c. expect to

Paraphrase 2. What does the sentence "When an elder dies, a library is burned" (line 19) mean?
a. When an elder dies, the people in the tribe start to forget them.
b. When old people who speak an endangered language die, lots of knowledge dies too.
c. People in some areas burn books when the leader of their tribe dies.

Detail 3. Harrison believes that ____ know about undiscovered animal species.
a. scientists   b. language experts   c. local tribes

Inference 4. According to the passage, who is most important in stopping language death?
a. elders   b. children   c. linguists

B **Strategy: Identifying fact and opinion.** Complete the statements below using one or two words from the passage. Then decide if each statement is a fact (**F**) or an opinion (**O**).

1. Languages die because they don't have as much ____ as other languages.
2. Endangered languages often aren't ____.
3. More common languages are more ____ for children to learn.
4. When languages die, we also lose ____ and histories of a group of people.
5. When we lose a language, we lose words that express ____ ideas.
6. If languages die, we lose knowledge about ____ and ecosystems.

A Quechua high school student in a language class, Peru.

Reading Comprehension questions check students' understanding of the reading passage.

Language Practice

A **Vocabulary: Words in context.** Answer the questions below. Share your answers with a partner.

1. Name three countries with a powerful **economy**.
2. What was the last question you didn't know how to **respond** to?
3. Do you prefer to **express** yourself in writing or by speaking?
4. How many hours a night do you think is the right **amount** of sleep?
5. What do you wish your teacher would **allow** you to do in class?
6. What are two **specific** things you want to do this year?
7. What **local** foods should visitors to your city try? Why?
8. Do you usually make decisions quickly, or do you **reflect** for a while first?

B **Grammar: Using furthermore.** Read the example sentences. Sentence a is from the passage.

a. Words that describe a cultural idea may not translate exactly into another language. **Furthermore**, many endangered languages have rich spoken cultures.
b. To begin with, language is a huge part of the culture of the people who speak it. **Furthermore**, language allows speakers to say specific things.

Complete the first sentence using **furthermore**. Then write three more sentences. Read your sentences with a partner.

1. I don't like ____. Furthermore ____
2. ____
3. ____
4. ____

Word Partners

Use **local** with:
(n.) local area, local artist, local business, local news, local office, local government, local police

Grammar activities practice important grammar structures introduced in the reading passage.

Vocabulary Builder boxes highlight common collocations, affixes, and usage notes.

102   8A Disappearing Languages   103

Reading Strategies give students the practice and support they need to be better readers.

Maps, **charts**, and **diagrams** help students develop visual literacy.

Before You Read tasks introduce eight target vocabulary items from the reading.

Target Vocabulary items from the readings are identified in blue.

Reading Comprehension questions include question types commonly found in international exams, such as TOEIC®, TOEFL®, and IELTS®.

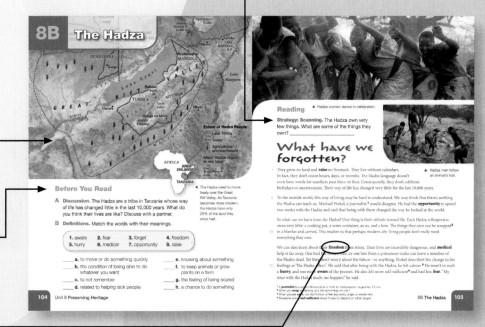

Vocabulary sections practice and reinforce target vocabulary from the reading.

Graphic organizers help students understand the organization of the text and the connections between key ideas.

Video activities give extra comprehension and vocabulary practice, and motivate students to learn more about the unit topic.

Review Unit Walkthrough

World Heritage Site
pages highlight important cultural and natural places around the world, and recycle vocabulary and structures from earlier units.

Vocabulary Review
activities reinforce the vocabulary from earlier units.

World Heritage Notes
preview content of World Heritage Site pages.

Folktales
from areas related to the World Heritage sites in the preceding spread introduce students to stories from cultures around the world.

Reading Comprehension
questions check students' understanding of the folktale.

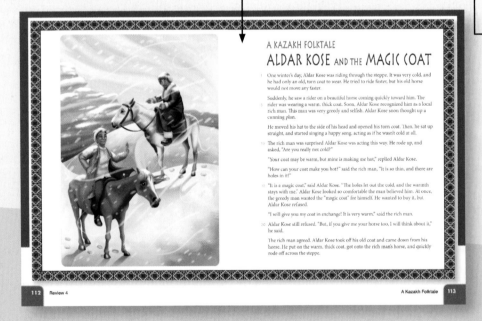

Make reading an adventure online—anywhere, any time! Visit **www.HeinleELT.com/readingadventures** for self-study grammar, vocabulary, and reading activities. Watch the National Geographic videos from the series either inside or outside the classroom.

Predators and Prey

◄ A pygmy seahorse uses camouflage to hide in the branches of a sea fan (a kind of coral).

Warm Up

Talk with a partner.

1. Animals use camouflage to look like the things around them. What are some animals that use camouflage?
2. What kind of dangers do animals face? What kind of things do they do to survive?

Hiding from Danger

line

leaf vein

▲ These leaf-litter toads look just like dead leaves.

Before You Read

A **Discussion.** Look at the picture above. Can you find the toads? With a partner, talk about other examples of camouflage you know.

B **Definitions.** Match the words (**1** to **8**) with their meanings (**a** to **h**).

> **1.** require   **2.** stay away   **3.** nearby   **4.** single
> **5.** overlook   **6.** scary   **7.** imitate   **8.** consider

_____ **a.** to think about

_____ **b.** close, a short distance away

_____ **c.** to need

_____ **d.** this describes something that makes you afraid

_____ **e.** one, only one

_____ **f.** to try to be like something else

_____ **g.** to not see something

_____ **h.** to not go near something, to avoid

Reading

Strategy: Scanning. Read the passage quickly. Which of these animals is not mentioned?

☐ snake   ☐ toad

☐ bug   ☐ turtle

ANiMAL CAMOUFLAGE

Two katydids in the forests of Panama look exactly like leaves.

1   A twig[1] suddenly flies by. Just as suddenly, it moves—then stops on a **nearby** tree. A vine moves slowly up a plant, and a brown leaf **hops** across the forest floor. Your eyes aren't playing tricks on you. The twig isn't really a twig—it's an insect. The green vine is a snake, and the jumping leaf is a leaf-litter toad. In the rain forest in Panama, things sometimes

5   **require** a closer look.

NATURE'S COPY CATS

Many animals **imitate** other animals or plants. Doing so makes them harder to see, and can sometimes mean the difference between life and death. To trick predators,[2] no detail can be **overlooked**. For example, the leaf-litter toad looks just like a leaf, right down to the line

10   down the toad's back, which looks like a leaf vein.

WORKING TOGETHER

Sometimes, animals work together to blend in.[3] **Consider** the thorn bug. One thorn bug looks like a **single** thorn[4]— not particularly **scary**. However, when many of the bugs sit

15   together on a branch, the branch looks thorny. As a result, other animals **stay away** from the branch, and the bugs.

Once you know how animals imitate others, you may begin to notice things that you did not see before. In nature, things are not

20   always what they seem.

One thorn bug doesn't have much ▲ protection against predators, but together, they look dangerous.

a **thorn bug**

[1] A **twig** is a small branch of a tree.
[2] A **predator** lives by killing and eating other animals.
[3] If something **blends in,** it looks like other things close by.
[4] A **thorn** is a sharp point on a plant.

Reading Comprehension

A Circle the correct answer.

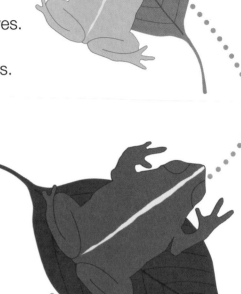

Main Idea **1.** What is the main idea of the passage?

    a. Some animals imitate nature to protect themselves.
    b. Some animals imitate nature to catch prey.
    c. Insects use camouflage better than other animals.

Gist **2.** In line 2, **hops** means _____.

    a. flies
    b. runs
    c. jumps

Detail **3.** In the first paragraph, the twig is actually _____.

    a. a snake
    b. a bird
    c. an insect

Vocabulary **4.** Which of these animals works in groups to use camouflage to avoid predators?

    a. the snake
    b. the thorn bug
    c. the toad

B **Strategy: Matching cause and effect.** Read the sentences. Match the cause to the effect.

1. A snake is long and thin.	○ ○	**a.** Animals think it's a leaf.
2. An insect is long and brown.	○ ○	**b.** Predators avoid them.
3. Animals copy nearby plants.	○ ○	**c.** It looks like a vine.
4. The toad has a line down its back.	○ ○	**d.** It looks like a twig.
5. Many bugs sit on a branch together.	○ ○	**e.** Predators cannot see them very easily.

Language Practice

A **Vocabulary: Completion.** Answer the questions below. Share your answers with a partner.

1. What is one thing that your school's rules **require** students to do?

2. Name something you try to **stay away** from.

3. In a restaurant, do you ever listen to the conversations of people sitting **nearby**?

4. Have you ever been to three or more cities in a **single** day?

5. Give an example of something you can **overlook**.

6. Name something you think is **scary**.

7. Can you **imitate** anyone famous?

8. What do you need to **consider** before you go to another country?

B **Grammar: Using *as a result*.** Read the example sentences. Sentence **a** is from the passage.

> **a. As a result**, other animals stay away from the branch, and the bugs.
>
> **b.** The leaf-litter toad looks just like a leaf. **As a result**, the toad tricks other animals.
>
> **c.** Several species became extinct **as a result of** forest clearing in the area.

Complete sentences 1 and 2. Then use **as a result** to write two more ideas.

1. Animals copy other animals or plants. As a result, _____ .

2. I studied English at school. As a result, _____ .

3. _____ .

4. _____ .

Usage

Require and *need* have similar meanings. In everyday conversation, *need* sounds more natural. E.g., *I **need** a coffee!*

Require is more formal. E.g., *Students are **required** to be at school by 8:30 a.m.*

Before You Read

▲ The argiope spider makes a web that looks like a flower to confuse insects.

A **Quiz.** How much do you know about spiders? Circle true (**T**) or false (**F**) for the sentences below. Then check your answers at the bottom of the page.

1.	Scientists know of over 35,000 spider species.	**T**	**F**
2.	Spider web is stronger than steel.	**T**	**F**
3.	Some spiders make webs up to five times a day.	**T**	**F**
4.	All spiders make webs to catch food.	**T**	**F**

B **Definitions.** Match the words with their meanings.

> **1.** material   **2.** combine   **3.** form (v.)   **4.** solid
> **5.** provide   **6.** confuse   **7.** realize   **8.** flexible

_____ **a.** not a liquid or gas

_____ **b.** to understand or come to know

_____ **c.** to make someone uncertain about something

_____ **d.** what something is made of

_____ **e.** to make something in a particular shape

_____ **f.** easily changed

_____ **g.** to make or give

_____ **h.** to make two things become one, to join

Answers: 1. T **2.** T. A piece of spider web thread is stronger than a piece of steel of the same weight. **3.** T. They eat the web, and then they make another one. **4.** F. Only female and young spiders make webs, and some species don't use webs to catch food at all.

Reading

Strategy: Predicting. What are some of the things that spiders can do with their webs? Make a list, then read the passage to see if any other uses are given.

DEADLY SILK

1   They weigh almost nothing, yet they are
    stronger than steel. In fact, some spiders'
    webs are among the world's strongest
    materials, but they stretch more than
5   elastic. They can also be any shape.
    Spider webs are amazing.

CHANGING FOR THE CONDITIONS

A spider's silk-making organ[1] has hundreds
of small openings. Silk comes out of these
10 openings as a liquid, and, as it reaches the
air, it becomes thread-like. These tiny threads
combine to **form** a single, **solid** thread.

The silver argiope spider catches a beetle in its web. ▲

The spider can make many different kinds
of thread. The threads can be thick or thin,
15 wet or dry, sticky or woolly. Each kind has a different purpose. Some webs create an egg case.[2]
Others **provide** hiding places. The most common purpose of a spider web, however, is
to catch food.

TRICKS FOR CATCHING DINNER

There are many ways the spider uses its web to catch prey. For example, some
20 spiders **spin** a single thread. An insect then sits on it without **realizing** what
it is doing, and becomes stuck. Slowly, the spider moves toward the
insect. Suddenly, it covers its prey in silk.

Argiope spiders use a different kind of trap. They make webs that
confuse insects. An insect sees the web and thinks it's a flower. It then lands
25 on the web. The spider can feel even the smallest movement of the web,
and rushes at the insect before it can get away.

Spider webs are so amazing that engineers have been studying **them** for years. They want
to learn why they are so strong and **flexible**. However, for the moment, spiders are keeping
their secrets. Despite their science and technology, humans still haven't been able to
30 copy natural webs.

[1] An **organ** is a part of the body that has a function, like your heart or eyes.
[2] An **egg case** protects spider eggs until the babies come out.

Reading Comprehension

A Circle the correct answer.

Gist **1.** The reading is mainly about the _____ of spider webs.

    a. beauty   **b.** human uses   **c.** different types and uses

Detail **2.** According to the passage, which of these statements about spider webs is true?

    a. A single thread is actually many smaller threads.
    b. Each kind of spider makes a single type of thread.
    c. Engineers use it instead of steel for some purposes.

Vocabulary **3.** In line 20, the word **spin** means _____.

    a. use   **b.** make   **c.** have

Inference **4.** In line 27, the word **them** refers to _____.

    a. engineers   **b.** natural webs   **c.** human-made materials

B **Strategy: Identifying supporting ideas.** Match each of the topics (**1–3**) with two of the supporting ideas (**a–f**).

Topics	Supporting Ideas
1. Spiders can make different webs for different purposes. _____ _____	**a.** Spider silk is one of the strongest materials in the world. **b.** A spider can feel even the smallest movement of its web.
2. Spiders catch prey using their webs. _____ _____	**c.** Some webs look like flowers and confuse insects. **d.** Sticky webs catch insects.
3. Humans can learn a lot from spider webs. _____ _____	**e.** Engineers want to know why spider silk can take so many different shapes. **f.** Sometimes a web is for hiding, but other times it is for holding eggs.

Water on the ▶
threads of a
spider web.

Language Practice

A Vocabulary: Words in context. Answer the questions below. Share your answers with a partner.

1. Do you think that schools should **provide** computers to their students?

2. What are some of the **materials** a car is made from?

3. Name something that is not **solid**.

4. Name something that you find **confusing**.

5. What is one thing you **realized** recently?

6. Name something you own that is very **flexible**.

7. How many different words can you **form** from the letters "a," "c," "h," and "t"?

8. If you **combine** two parts hydrogen (H) and one part oxygen (O), what do you get?

B Grammar: Using *among*. Read the example sentences. Sentence **a** is from the passage.

> **a**. Some spiders' webs are **among** the world's strongest materials.
>
> **b**. A leaf-litter toad is **among** those leaves.
>
> **c. Among** researchers, there is a lot of debate on that issue.

Complete the sentences with your ideas. Compare answers with a partner.

1. Among all the different kinds of fruit, I like _____ the best.

2. At home, my family speaks _____ among themselves.

3. Among all the animals, I think _____.

4. Among my family and friends, _____.

▲ A Carolina wolf spider wraps a beetle in its web.

A **Preview.** Are the statements below true (**T**) or false (**F**). Discuss your answers with a partner.

1. Spider silk is about the same thickness as human hair.   **T   F**

2. A thread of spider silk stretched all the way around the Earth   **T   F**
   would weigh more than 1,000 kilograms.

3. Some spiders are able to catch bats in their webs.   **T   F**

4. Some spiders catch their prey by throwing their webs like nets.   **T   F**

5. Spiders always eat their prey right away.   **T   F**

B **After you watch.** Check your answers to the statements in **A**. If a statement was false, rewrite it to make it true.

C **Think about it.** Did any of the information in the video surprise you? Tell a partner.

◀ A bionic leg helps a man with a missing leg run again.

Warm Up

Talk with a partner.

1. Bionic body parts are made by humans. Have you ever heard of someone with a bionic body part?
2. Would you like to have any bionic body parts? If so, which ones?

Remaking Humans

Before You Read

▲ Amanda Kitts, who lost her arm in a car accident,[1] shows her new artificial[2] arm.

A Discussion. Amanda Kitts is one of "tomorrow's people"—people who have artificial body parts. What do you know about artificial body parts? Talk about your ideas with a partner.

B Definitions. Match the words with their meanings.

> **1.** angry **2.** surround **3.** control **4.** operation
> **5.** accept **6.** bend **7.** rough **8.** remain

_____ **a.** to make something work in the way you want

_____ **b.** to stay or be left

_____ **c.** to take something; to agree with an idea

_____ **d.** feeling strong dislike and impatience

_____ **e.** when a doctor cuts into someone for medical reasons

_____ **f.** not smooth

_____ **g.** to move the top part of your body downwards and forwards

_____ **h.** to be on every side of something

[1] An **accident** is a sudden, unplanned event that hurts someone or something.
[2] If something is **artificial**, humans made it, not nature.

Reading

Strategy: Predicting.
Without reading the passage, what do you think Kitts can do with her bionic arm? What do you think she can't do?

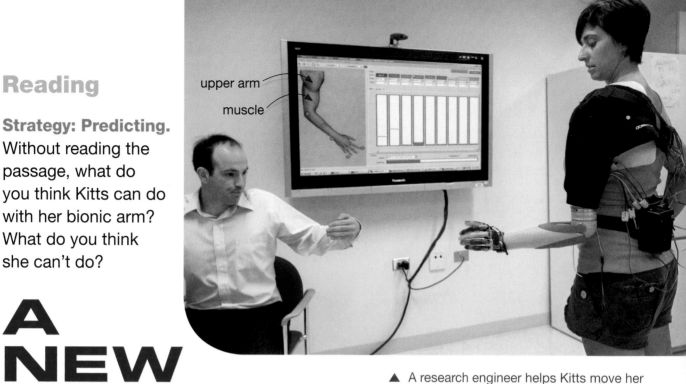

upper arm

muscle

▲ A research engineer helps Kitts move her new arm in a more natural way.

A NEW START

1   Children **surround** Amanda Kitts as she comes into the classroom. She **bends** over to talk with a small girl. As she bends, Kitts puts her hands on her knees. For most people, this wouldn't be extraordinary. However, just a few years ago,
5   this was impossible for Kitts.

In 2006, Kitts—who runs a day-care center¹—was in a car accident. A truck crushed² her arm. "I was **angry**, sad, depressed. I just couldn't **accept** it," she says. But then she heard about a new technique³ that could use the **remaining**
10   nerves in her shoulder to **control** an artificial arm.

▲ Kitts uses her artificial arm to unlock a door.

In a difficult **operation**, a surgeon moved Kitts's nerves to different areas of her upper-arm muscles. For months, the nerves grew. Millimeter by millimeter, they moved deeper into their new homes. "At three months I started feeling little **tingles and twitches**," she said. A month later, she got her first bionic arm. A research engineer worked with Kitts to make the computer
15   programs match her real movements more and more closely.

Today, Kitts's arm is great, but it's not yet perfect. She wants feeling in her hands. For example, she needs to feel whether something is **rough** or smooth. She also needs feeling to do one of her favorite things—drink coffee. "The problem with a paper coffee cup is that my hand will close until it gets a solid grip," she says. One time at a coffee shop, her hand kept closing until
20   it crushed the cup. But Kitts says positively, "One day I'll be able to feel things with it . . . and clap my hands . . . to the songs my kids are singing."

¹ A **day-care center** is a place that looks after young children when their parents are at work.
² When you **crush** something, you push it very hard so it breaks or changes shape.
³ A **technique** is a way to do something, usually with special knowledge.

Reading Comprehension

A Circle the correct answer.

Detail   **1.** Which word best describes Kitts's attitude toward her new arm?

     a. positive   **b.** angry   **c.** confused

Vocabulary   **2.** In line 13, the phrase **tingles and twitches** describes the sense of _____.

     a. touch   **b.** sight   **c.** hearing

Detail   **3.** With her bionic hand, Kitts _____.

     a. can feel everything   **b.** can feel some things   **c.** can't feel anything

Inference   **4.** What is Kitts able to do with her bionic arm?

     a. clap her hands   **b.** hold things   **c.** feel rough things

B   **Strategy: Sequencing.** Number the events in order from **1** to **6**.

     a. _____ Kitts heard about a new kind of operation.

     b. _____ Kitts crushed a paper coffee cup.

     c. _____ Kitts had two human arms.

     d. _____ A truck hit Kitts's car.

     e. _____ Kitts got her first bionic arm.

     f. _____ Doctors moved some of the nerves in Kitts's arm.

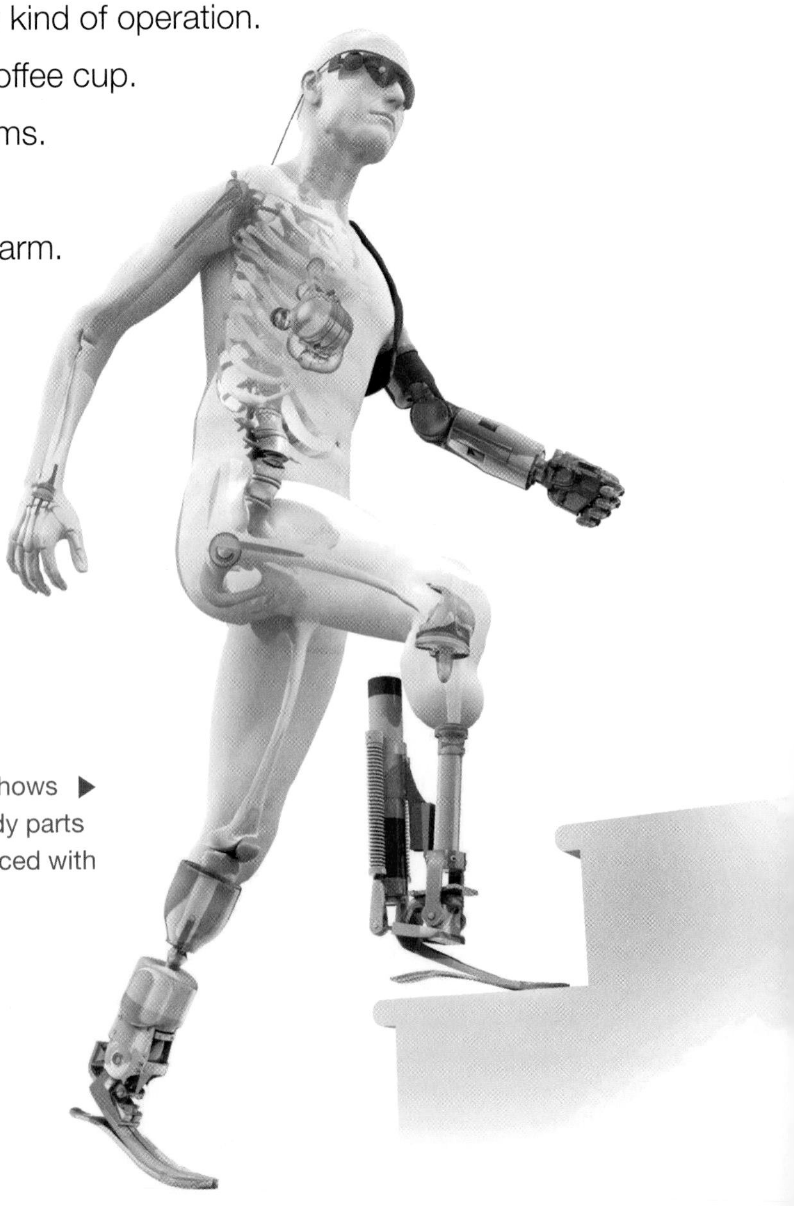

This illustration shows ▶ the variety of body parts that can be replaced with bionic versions.

Language Practice

A **Vocabulary: Words in context.** In each sentence, (circle) the best answer.

1. People who are (**angry** / **sad**) often yell.[1]

2. Australia is (**overlooked** / **surrounded**) by water.

3. A good basketball player has to (**control** / **combine**) the ball.

4. Surgeons are doctors who do (**tricks** / **operations**).

5. When someone asks, "Do you want this?" and you say, "Yes, thank you," you (**agree** / **accept**) it.

6. You can (**bend** / **stretch**) the branch of a tree.

7. A ribbon is not (**rough** / **smooth**).

8. Lonesome George, a tortoise in the Galapagos Islands, is the world's most endangered animal. He is the only (**realizing** / **remaining**) one of his kind.

B **Grammar: Using *whether*.** Read the example sentences. Sentence **a** is from the passage.

> **a.** She needs to feel **whether** something is rough or smooth.
>
> **b.** The spider chooses **whether** to make threads thick or thin.
>
> **c.** I can't decide **whether or not** to go to the party on Friday.

Complete the sentences with your own ideas, and write two more sentences. Then read them to a partner.

1. In the future, I may have to choose whether _____.

2. I can't decide whether or not _____.

3. _____.

4. _____.

> ## Word Partners
>
> **Use *bend* with:**
> (*adv.*) bend **backward/forward**, bend **down**, bend **over**
> (*n.*) bend **your arms/knees**, bend **the rules**
> (*prep.*) **around the** bend, bend **in a river/road**

[1] When you **yell**, you shout or scream.

Making Robots Human

Before You Read

▲ This robot from Osaka University, Japan, learns like a human child—by watching and talking to humans.

A Discussion. Imagine you could make a robot. What would you want it to do? Talk about your ideas with a partner.

B Definitions. Match the words with their meanings.

> **1.** generation   **2.** independent   **3.** develop   **4.** industry
> **5.** increase   **6.** prove   **7.** shrink   **8.** fold

_____ **a.** to bend something so that one part covers another part

_____ **b.** to become larger

_____ **c.** to create something, usually over a period of time

_____ **d.** to become smaller

_____ **e.** the work of making things, e.g. in a factory

_____ **f.** not needing other people

_____ **g.** all the people in a group or country who are of a similar age

_____ **h.** to show something is true or correct

Reading

Strategy: Scanning.
Quickly read the introduction. What are some things robots are probably going to start doing for the first time?

THEM AND US

▲ a robot soccer team from Virginia Tech, U.S.A.

1 Robots are already popular in **industry**, but scientists and engineers around the world are now **developing** a new **generation** of robots. These new robots are becoming **increasingly independent**. They can cook and clean, and may soon
5 even take care of young children and older people. In the future, they will do things that only humans did before. This new generation of robots may be more like friends or family members than machines.

ROBOTIC HELP

New robots are no longer just machines. They are now able to do
10 things they never did in the past. PR2, for example, is a prototype[1] of such a robot. At the company that created it, PR2 delivers mail, but it is also able to cook and **fold** laundry. It can even be programmed to help older people. "In five to ten years, robots will routinely[2] be functioning in human environments," Reid Simmons,
15 a professor of robotics, predicts.

SPENDING TIME TOGETHER

Hiroshi Ishiguro is a robot expert. He wants to make robots more **realistic**. He believes the differences between humans and robots will continue to **shrink** until people think of them as human.

▲ Hiroshi Ishiguro's robot twin

20 Ishiguro is trying to **prove** this using a robotic twin[3] he has built. While most of us may dream of having a robot to do our work for us, Ishiguro has a different idea. He thinks the best use for his twin would be at his mother's home. She lives far away, and he is rarely able to visit her. But if she had a robot, she could spend more time with "him." When asked why his mother would be happy with a robot son, he replies, "Because it is myself."

25 If robots become enough like people that you can't tell the difference, Ishiguro wonders, "does it really matter if you're interacting with a human or machine?"

---

[1] A **prototype** is something that is being developed and tested before it is sold.
[2] When we do things **routinely**, we do them regularly.
[3] A **twin** is one of two children born to the same mother at the same time.

Reading Comprehension

A Circle the correct answer.

Detail **1.** According to the passage, robots are becoming more and more _____ .

    a. like humans   **b.** like machines   **c.** dependent on people

Detail **2.** Right now, most people _____ robots like PR2.

    a. can buy and use   **b.** are unlikely to see   **c.** are increasingly likely to see

Vocabulary **3.** In line 18, the word **realistic** means _____ .

    a. human-like   **b.** with more abilities   **c.** helpful

Inference **4.** Ishiguro probably _____ .

    a. sees his mother less often than she would like

    b. thinks robots are dangerous

    c. thinks that everyone will own a robot in the future

B **Strategy: Identifying fact and opinion.** Which of these statements about robots are facts (**F**), and which are opinions (**O**)? With a partner, talk about which opinions you agree with and why.

_____ **a.** The new generation of robots will take care of people.

_____ **b.** Robots are becoming more like humans.

_____ **c.** In 2020, people will think of robots as their friends.

_____ **d.** Spending time with a robot is as good as spending time with a human.

_____ **e.** In the future, robots will be able to do things that only humans can do now.

Years ago, robot ▶
expert Nick Mayer
wouldn't have
imagined sitting
down for a chat
with a robotic
head, but it's no
longer something
from science
fiction.

Language Practice

A Vocabulary: Words in context. In each sentence, circle the best answer.

1. A woman and her _____ are part of the same **generation**.
   a. son   **b.** sister

2. Which of these is more **independent**?
   a. an adult   **b.** a baby

3. Which of these do athletes try to **develop**?
   a. team uniforms   **b.** their abilities

4. Which of these is part of the food **industry**?
   a. restaurants   **b.** salads

5. Do children **shrink** as they get older?
   a. Yes.   **b.** No.

6. Scientists use _____ to **prove** something is true.
   a. discussions   **b.** experiments

7. The number of people in the world _____ **increasing**.
   a. is   **b.** isn't

8. You can **fold** a _____.
   a. ruler   **b.** shirt

B Grammar: *If* to talk about imaginary situations. Read the example sentences. Sentence **a** is from the passage.

> **a. If** she had a robot, she **could** spend more time with "him."
>
> **b. If** Kitts could feel things with her hands, she **could** drink from a paper cup.
>
> **c. If** I studied more, I **would** have higher grades.

Complete the sentences. Then write two more sentences using **if**.

1. If I had more money, I would _____.

2. If I could do anything, I'd _____.

3. _____.

4. _____.

Word Partners

Use *fold* with:
(adv.) fold **carefully**, fold **gently**, fold **neatly**
(n.) fold **clothes**, fold **paper**, fold **your arms**

Bionic Eyes

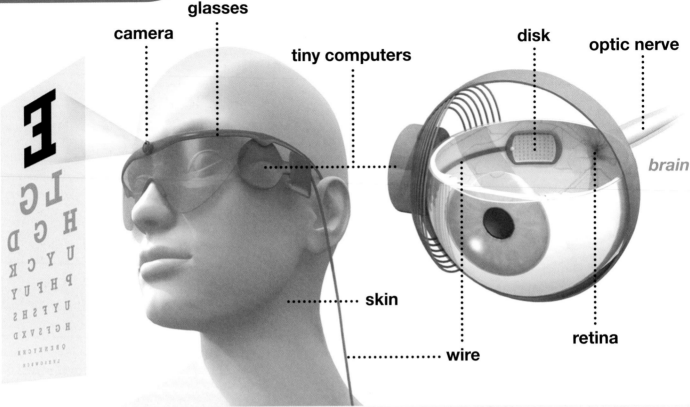

glasses
camera
tiny computers
disk
optic nerve
brain
skin
retina
wire

A Preview. Lynda Morfot lost her eyesight ten years ago. Read her quote below. How do you think she feels? Discuss with a partner.

"It's frustrating to lose your sight because you run into things, you run into people. You trip over things. It's just frustrating."

B After you watch. Look at the diagram showing how the bionic eye works. Complete the statements below using labels from the diagram.

1. A _____ in the glasses looks at the world and turns light into electrical signals.

2. The signal goes to a small computer, which then sends it wirelessly to another computer under her _____.

3. From there, the signal travels along a thin _____ to a disk on her _____.

4. The optic nerve carries signals from the retina to the _____.

C Think about it. Do you think there might be problems if bionic body parts become common? If so, what kind of problems?

Vocabulary Review

A **Odd word out.** One word in each group is a different part of speech to the others. Circle the different words.

1. generation   provide   operation
2. develop   nearby   overlook
3. imitate   increase   industry
4. angry   independent   require
5. rough   remain   realize
6. material   operation   accept
7. surround   scary   single
8. form   fold   flexible

B **Word search.** Now look for the words you circled, and find them in the puzzle.

Y	R	T	S	U	D	N	I	E
I	H	E	A	Y	N	I	P	L
R	I	G	R	U	U	L	E	B
U	N	D	U	X	O	Q	N	I
E	D	I	V	O	R	P	E	X
R	E	Q	U	I	R	E	A	E
I	P	Y	S	S	U	E	R	L
Y	U	Y	U	D	S	H	B	F
A	C	C	E	P	T	S	Y	F

World Heritage Notes

Notes completion. Scan the information on pages 32 and 33 to complete the notes.

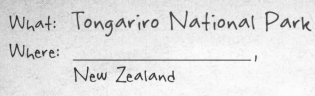

What: Tongariro National Park

Where: _____,
       New Zealand

Data:

• Tongariro is the _____ national park in New Zealand.

• The park is made of mostly _____ environments.

• In the park, there are _____, ski fields, _____, and lakes.

• The park has three _____, which are important in the culture of the _____ people.

• Animals that live in the park include the _____ and the _____.

• The _____ is the national symbol of New Zealand.

Tongariro National Park

Site: **Tongariro National Park**

Location: **Central North Island, New Zealand**

Category: **Mixed (Natural and Cultural)**

Status: **World Heritage Site since 1990**

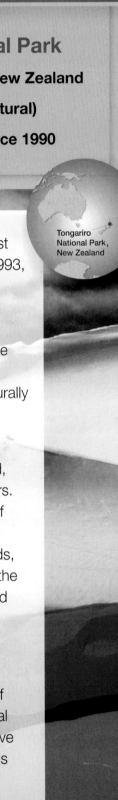

Tongariro
National Park,
New Zealand

Tongariro National Park is the oldest national park in New Zealand. In 1993, it became the first World Heritage Site to be recognized as a cultural landscape. This means it contains natural environments that should be protected both because they are unique, and because they are culturally important to the native people.

The park, located near the center of the North Island of New Zealand, covers about 800 square kilometers. It protects various different types of landscape. There are mountaintop glaciers and snow-covered ski fields, hot springs and lakes that form in the craters of the park's volcanoes, and lush areas of rain forest.

At the center of the park are three huge active volcanoes—Ruapehu, Ngauruhoe, and Tongariro. Each of these peaks have important cultural and religious meanings for the native Maori people, who have lived in this area for about a thousand years.

The kiwi, which lives only in New Zealand, is the country's national symbol. This North Island brown kiwi lives in Tongariro National Park. There are only about 35,000 brown kiwis left on Earth.

One of New Zealand's most distinctive insect species, the giant weta is one of the largest insects in the world. They can grow up to 20 cm in length, and weigh up to 71 grams.

One legend says that when the Maori people first arrived in New Zealand from Polynesia, a high priest named Ngatoroirangi was frozen in a snowstorm while exploring Mount Tongariro. He called out to his sisters in Hawaiki—the traditional Polynesian homeland of the Maori—for fire. His prayer was answered; the fire came, and Mount Tongariro erupted. But as the fire traveled to Tongariro, it also created a whole series of volcanoes, which stretched from Polynesia to New Zealand. This series of volcanoes is what we now call the Pacific Rim of Fire.

Maui and the Magic Fishhook

1   Once upon a time, there was a young demi-god called Maui, who had many magical powers. Maui dreamed of the day that he could go fishing with his older brothers. But each time he asked, they would refuse. "You're too young," they said.

5   Maui really wanted to go with them; he wanted to prove he was a good fisherman. So, one day, he hid in the bottom of his brothers' fishing boat. After they had rowed out to sea, the brothers discovered Maui hiding in the boat. They wanted to take him back to shore, but Maui used his powers to make the shore seem very far away. Because they thought returning to shore would take
10 a long time, Maui's brothers decided to let him stay.

When they were in the middle of the ocean, the brothers started to catch fish. Maui took out a magic fishhook that he had gotten from his grandmother, a sorceress. He attached it to his fishing line, and threw it into the water.

After a while, there was a strong pull on Maui's line. He tried to pull in the
15 line, but whatever he had caught was too strong. Maui had to ask his brothers for help. They pulled and pulled. Finally, they pulled up a huge piece of land, which is now known as the North Island of New Zealand.

Today, the symbol of Maui's magic—his fishhook—has become an important symbol to the Maori people, who believe wearing *Hei Matau* (fishhook
20 necklaces) will keep them safe on their travels and bring them wealth. And in the Maori language, the piece of land that Maui caught is still called *Te Ika a Maui*, meaning *Maui's fish*.

Reading Comprehension

Circle the correct answer.

1. Maui's brothers were older than him.   T   F
2. Maui made the shore seem further away than it really was.   T   F
3. The fishhook was a present from Maui's father.   T   F
4. Maui's eldest brother caught the North Island.   T   F
5. The Maori believe wearing *Hei Matau* will bring them wealth. T   F

Language Extension

Vocabulary: Word web. Using words from the folktale on page 35, complete the word web about fishing. Then using a different topic, make a word web of your own.

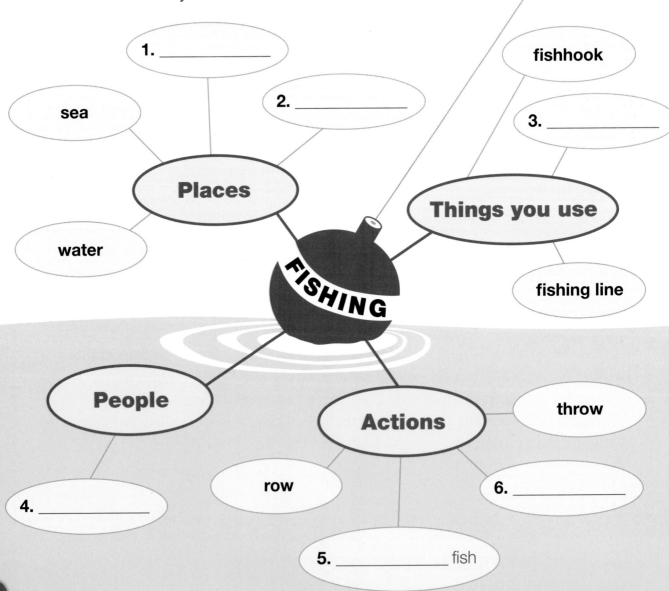

Clues about the Past

Billions of years ago, the Earth looked very similar to this volcano in Hawaii.

Warm Up

Talk with a partner.

1. Do you think life could survive in a place like the one in the photo? Why or why not?

2. What do you think scientists can learn about Earth's history from a place like this?

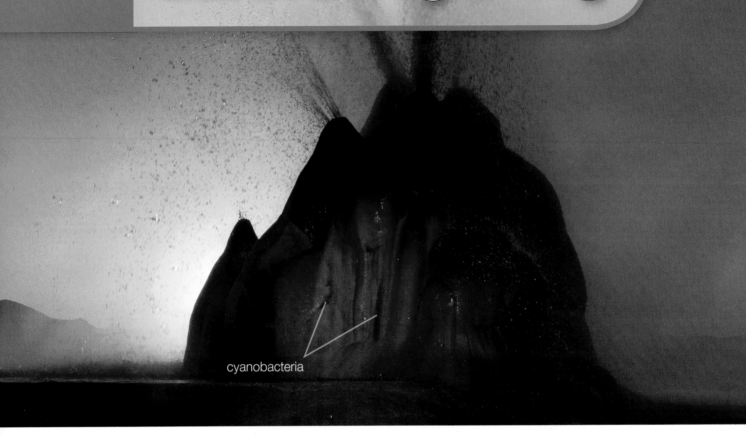

cyanobacteria

▲ Boiling water comes out of a natural geyser in Nevada, U.S.A. Cyanobacteria leave blue-green streaks on the wet area.

Before You Read

A Discussion. What do you know about the beginning of the Earth? Talk about your ideas with your partner.

B Definitions. Match the words with their meanings.

1. level	**2.** rise	**3.** exist	**4.** appear
5. series	**6.** process	**7.** within	**8.** recognize

_____ **a.** to increase, to move upwards

_____ **b.** events that happen one after the other

_____ **c.** actions that make something happen

_____ **d.** how much there is of something

_____ **e.** in; inside

_____ **f.** to know who or what something is

_____ **g.** to start to be; to become visible

_____ **h.** to live; to be real

Reading

Strategy: Predicting.
Where did life on Earth first appear—on land or in the sea? Read the passage to check your answer.

The Road to Life

stromatolites in Shark Bay, Australia

1 Scientists generally think the Earth came into **existence** 4.6 billion years ago. If you could have seen it back then, you wouldn't

5 have **recognized** it; it wouldn't have looked anything like the Earth we know now. So what did it look like? And how did the Earth start to support life?

For the first 700 million years, huge pieces of solid rock floated in a sea of magma—the same magma that comes out

10 of volcanoes as lava today. This cooling magma released water vapor,[1] creating the oceans. However, there was no oxygen, and the air couldn't support life.

Then, about 3.5 billion years ago, single-celled blue-green cyanobacteria started to exist. Originally, they survived on

15 chemicals[2] **within** the water. However, slowly they changed. Over time, **they** developed the ability to turn energy from the sun into food. Little by little, the cyanobacteria helped turn the atmosphere into breathable air.

▲ The first land plants were similar to this whisk fern, in Hawaii, U.S.A.

Stromatolites were also living on Earth 3.5 billion years ago. Part rock and part living things, they also helped create Earth's breathable air. By about 2.4 billion years ago, the **level** of oxygen

20 in the atmosphere[3] had **risen** enough for other things to live.

Scientists believe the very first land plants **appeared**, and produced oxygen, around 470 million years ago—millions of years before the first reptiles and mammals. At first, the plants were small and grew slowly. Over time, however, the plants developed stronger stems. Little by little, they grew taller and bigger.

25 Earth has seen an amazing **series** of changes. We can still see these **processes** today. For example, volcanoes still erupt, creating new land, and plants continue to make oxygen— just as they have for billions of years.

[1] **Vapor** is tiny drops of water or other liquids in the air.
[2] **Chemicals** are the substances that combine and react to form other substances.
[3] The **atmosphere** is all of the air surrounding Earth.

Reading Comprehension

A Circle the correct answer.

Detail **1.** Which of these helped make water for the oceans?

    a. magma

    b. the changing of energy into food

    c. living things like cyanobacteria and stromatolites

Reference **2.** In line 15, **they** refers to _____.

    a. stromatolites   **b.** chemicals   **c.** cyanobacteria

Detail **3.** It took about _____ years before there was enough oxygen in the air for things to live.

    a. 2.2 billion   **b.** 2.4 billion   **c.** 3.5 billion

Detail **4.** Which of these slowly became stronger after moving onto land?

    a. cyanobacteria   **b.** stromatolites   **c.** plants

B **Strategy: Sequencing.** Put these events in order. Write **a** to **e** on the timeline.

    a. cyanobacteria and stromatolites appeared

    b. first land plants appeared

    c. magma cooled, releasing water vapor into the air

    d. the Earth formed

    e. oxygen levels in the atmosphere increased enough to support a greater variety of life

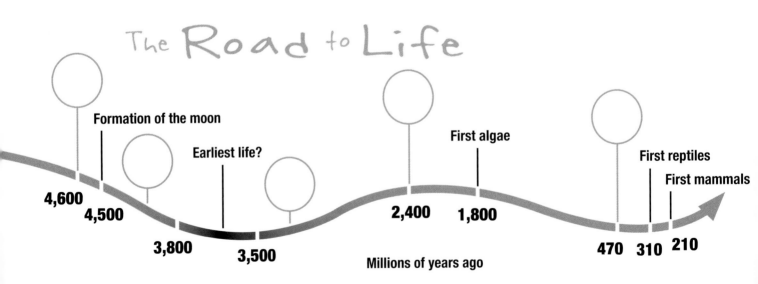

The Road to Life

Formation of the moon

Earliest life?

First algae

First reptiles

First mammals

4,600

4,500

3,800

3,500

2,400 1,800

470 310 210

Millions of years ago

Language Practice

A Vocabulary: Words in context. Match the two halves of the sentences.

1. A **series** of changes ○   ○ **a.** about 65 million years ago.

2. Dinosaurs **existed** until ○   ○ **b.** you can look at their photo.

3. There are many doctors ○   ○ **c.** makes your body temperature **rise**.

4. Playing table tennis ○   ○ **d.** **within** a hospital building.

5. Most people think CO_2 **levels** ○   ○ **e.** in the atmosphere are increasing.

6. The first animals **appeared** long after ○   ○ **f.** gave the atmosphere enough oxygen for life.

7. The **process** to change sea water ○   ○ **g.** the world began.

8. To **recognize** someone you've never met before, ○   ○ **h.** into water we can drink is expensive.

B Grammar: *If* to talk about imaginary past situations.
Read the example sentences. Sentence **a** is from the passage.

> **a.** **If** you **could have seen** it back then, you **wouldn't have recognized** it.
>
> **b.** **If** I **had practiced** more, I **could have won** the game.
>
> **c.** **If** Ishiguro **had developed** his robot twin many years ago, his mother **wouldn't have been** alone all these years.

Complete sentences 1–3 using your own ideas. Then write your own sentence. Share your answers with a partner.

1. If I had known _____.

2. If I had _____.

3. If I hadn't _____.

4. _____.

Word Partners

Use *process* with:
(adv.) **difficult** process, **long** process, **slow** process, **normal** process
(v.) **participate in a** process, **begin a** process, **complete a** process, **describe a** process

3B Deep Sea Vents

▲ Two kilometers deep in the Pacific Ocean, a deep sea vent supports a wide variety of life, including tube worms, crabs, and eelpout fish.

Before You Read

A Quiz. What do you know about the ocean? Circle True (**T**) or False (**F**) for the sentences below. Then check your answers at the bottom of the page.

1. The deepest point in the sea is in the Atlantic Ocean.   **T   F**

2. No human has ever gone to the deepest point in the sea.   **T   F**

3. One out of every six species lives in the ocean.   **T   F**

B Definitions. Match the words with their meanings.

> **1.** emphasize   **2.** expect   **3.** beyond   **4.** absolutely
>
> **5.** surface   **6.** hope   **7.** investigate   **8.** reason

_____ **a.** on the other side of

_____ **b.** to try to get information about something

_____ **c.** completely; 100%

_____ **d.** to say strongly; to give extra attention to

_____ **e.** the outside or top part of something

_____ **f.** to think; to believe something will happen

_____ **g.** to want something to be true or happen

_____ **h.** a fact that says why something is

1. F. It's in the Pacific Ocean. 2. F. Two men first went there in 1960. More recently, filmmaker James Cameron went there alone in 2012. 3. T. We know about 1.5 million species on Earth, and 250,000 of these are in the ocean.

Reading

▲ These sea stars are one of the species scientists found near the vents. They have "arms" that catch tiny pieces of food in the water.

Strategy: Scanning. Read the text quickly. When did scientists first find the deep sea vents? _____

DAWN OF THE DEEP

1   Imagine a place almost two kilometers below the sea **surface**. It's always dark—there is **absolutely** no sunlight. Scientists used to think that animals couldn't live without the sun's energy. As a result, they never **expected** to find living creatures **down there**. But they did.

CHANGING OLD iDEAS

5   In 1977, scientists got a surprise. Something was bubbling at the bottom of the ocean. They had found deep sea vents, home to amazing and unusual animals. Jonathan Eisen, one of the scientists **investigating** the vents, **emphasized** the discovery's importance. "It told us that life can thrive.[1] Not just grow a little bit, but actually thrive—[even]in the absence[2] of light." The vents are home to a huge number of creatures. On average, scientists have discovered a new
10   species every 10 days since 1979. Timothy Shank, a marine ecologist, calls the number of new species "mind-boggling." "We're still on the tip of the iceberg," he says.

THE VALUE OF THE DISCOVERY

The discovery was important for another **reason**. Scientists used to think animals couldn't live in temperatures above 55°C.[3] But the deep sea vents are that hot—sometimes even hotter. The
15   discovery of life in such an extreme environment made scientists review some of their ideas about the places in which life is possible. They **hope** the vents will give them more information about early life on Earth. Other scientists are looking into space. They believe that if life can survive in the vents, it might give us hope to find life **beyond** Earth.

[1] If something **thrives**, it does well.   [3] 55°C = 130°F
[2] Something's **absence** is the fact that it isn't there.

Reading Comprehension

A Circle the correct answer.

Detail **1.** Which of these best describes the environment of the deep sea vents?

    a. darkness and heat   **b.** sunlight and energy   **c.** cold and ice

Reference **2.** In line 3, the phrase **down there** refers to _____.

    a. deep inside the Earth   **b.** the Earth's surface   **c.** the bottom of the sea

Inference **3.** We can infer that Eisen believes finding the deep sea vents was _____.

    a. extremely disappointing **b.** somewhat surprising **c.** something he'd expected

Paraphrase **4.** The sentence "We're still on the tip of the iceberg" (line 11) means they _____.

    a. are standing on an iceberg
    b. still have a lot to discover
    c. have found most of the species near the vents

B **Strategy: Classification.** Which period of time do these sentences describe? Write **a** to **f** in the correct place.

    a. Scientists thought animals needed the sun's energy in order to survive.

    b. Scientists studied creatures in the ocean.

    c. Scientists believed animals only lived in temperatures below 55°C.

    d. Scientists found one new species every ten days, on average.

    e. Amazing animals lived around deep sea vents.

    f. Scientists explored the vents.

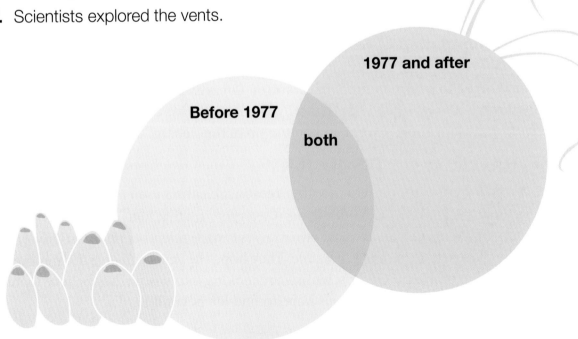

1977 and after

Before 1977

both

Language Practice

A Vocabulary: Completion. Complete the sentences using the words in the box.

> emphasize   expect   beyond   absolutely
> surface   hope   investigating   reasons

1. Oceans cover 70% of the Earth's _____ .

2. There were at least two _____ why scientists didn't think animals could live deep in the ocean.

3. Scientists _____ to find a cure for deadly diseases, but no one knows if they can.

4. Most teachers _____ their students to study hard.

5. The police are _____ the robbery carefully.

6. "Did you make this cake yourself? It's _____ delicious!"

7. Doctors _____ the importance of eating well if we want to be healthy.

8. It is difficult to predict the weather _____ the next few days.

B Grammar: Using *used to*. Read the example sentences. Sentence **a** is from the passage.

> **a.** Scientists **used to** think animals couldn't live in temperatures above 55°C.
>
> **b.** The Earth's atmosphere **didn't use to** contain oxygen.

Complete the sentences with your ideas. Compare answers with a partner.

1. _____ used to be more expensive than they are now.

2. _____ used to be popular, but isn't so much today.

3. I used to _____ .

4. I didn't use to _____ , but I do now.

Usage

Hope and *expect* both talk about future events, but have different meanings.

If you **hope** something happens, you want it to happen, but don't know if it will or not. E.g. *I* **hope** *it's sunny this afternoon; I forgot my umbrella.*

If you **expect** something will happen, you think it will happen. E.g. *Scientists* **expect** *to find more species near the vents in the next few years.*

▲ crabs and worms living near a deep sea vent

A Preview. Read the quote from the video below. It is from Bob Ballard, a deep sea explorer. Why do you think he says this? Discuss with a partner.

"What is amazing to me is that we didn't go into the largest feature on Earth until after [we] went to the moon. In fact, now we have better maps of Mars than we have of the deep sea beneath the waves."

B After you watch. Complete the summary of the video using the words in the box.

hot	humans	largest	life	light
microbes	robots	space	survive	tiny

Deep below the sea, scientists are exploring a strange new world called the Lost City. This place is in a group of undersea mountains—the **1.** _____ natural feature on Earth! The water here is extremely **2.** _____, and there is no **3.** _____, so scientists never expected to find **4.** _____ here.

Because **5.** _____ aren't able to visit the Lost City, researchers like Bob Ballard use **6.** _____ to learn about the place. Surprisingly, they have found a very large number of animals here. The reason they are able to **7.** _____ is because they eat **8.** _____ creatures called **9.** _____. The discovery of life in such an unlikely place has made scientists wonder whether it is possible that life could exist in **10.** _____.

C Think about it. Do you think it is important to spend money on exploring places like the deep sea and outer space? Why or why not? Discuss with a partner.

Survival

a mountain rescue team in Arizona, U.S.A.

Warm Up

Talk with a partner.

1. What is the most dangerous thing that has ever happened to you? What happened?

2. Think of a disaster you know about. How did people survive?

4A When Danger Is Near

▲ Madidi National Park, Bolivia

Before You Read

A **Discussion.** Look at the picture and read the information below. Do you think you could survive in Ghinsberg's situation? Discuss with a partner.

Madidi National Park, Bolivia, is one of the largest national parks in the world. In 1982, Yossi Ghinsberg, a young Swiss traveler, had to survive alone in the rain forest there for almost three weeks.

B **Definitions.** Match the words with their meanings.

> **1.** give up   **2.** end up   **3.** head (*v.*)   **4.** crisis
> **5.** explain   **6.** attitude   **7.** skill   **8.** go wrong

_____ **a.** technique; ability

_____ **b.** a bad situation that may get worse

_____ **c.** to stop being good; to start having problems

_____ **d.** ideas and feelings about something

_____ **e.** to quit or stop doing something

_____ **f.** to find yourself in a situation that was not planned

_____ **g.** to make something easy to understand

_____ **h.** to go toward

Reading

Strategy: Skimming. Quickly read the passage. What do Jerry Long and Yossi Ghinsberg have in common?

How to Survive Almost Anything

▲ Jerry Long

▲ Yossi Ghinsberg

1 What would you do if you got lost on a mountain? Could you survive a deadly natural disaster?[1] No one wants to find themselves in dangerous situations[2] like these. However,
5 developing survival **skills** can help you be prepared for whatever happens.

Stay Positive

People who believe they have control over what happens to them are more likely to believe in
10 themselves and take action. Jerry Long is a good example. When he was 17 years old, he broke his neck in a diving[3] accident. As a result, he couldn't move most of his body, and he had to hold a stick between his teeth to type. In the same situation, many
15 people might **give up**. Long, however, said that his life remained full of **meaning and purpose**. He said, "I broke my neck, it didn't break me."

Don't wait for a horrible situation. Start to develop **this** positive **attitude** today. Then, you'll be better prepared for anything.

Focus on Survival

20 Four young people **headed** into the middle of the Amazon rain forest. They thought they were on an amazing adventure, but then things started to **go wrong**. One of the adventurers, Yossi Ghinsberg, **ended up** alone and lost in the Bolivian jungle for three weeks. During that time, he repeated the phrase "man of action" to motivate[4] himself. Later, he **explained** it like this. "A man of action does whatever he must, isn't afraid, and doesn't worry."

25 If you find yourself in a **crisis**, first focus on survival. Everything else will take care of itself later.

---

[1] A **disaster** is something that happens suddenly and causes a lot of problems, such as a hurricane or earthquake.
[2] A **situation** is what is generally happening in a particular place at a particular time.
[3] When you **dive**, you jump into water head-first.
[4] If you **motivate** someone, you give them a reason to do something, or make them want to do it.

Reading Comprehension

A Circle the correct answer.

Detail **1.** Both Long and Ghinsberg would agree that, in a crisis, your _____ is the most important thing.

    a. preparation   **b.** attitude   **c.** equipment

Paraphrase **2.** In line 16, the phrase **meaning and purpose** means _____.

    a. explanations   **b.** reasons to live   **c.** understanding

Reference **3.** Which statement is Jerry Long most likely to agree with?

    a. You should wait for things to happen to you before worrying.
    b. You should give up when things are hard.
    c. You should try to take control of your situation.

Inference **4.** Ghinsberg probably thinks _____ is the most important thing in a crisis.

    a. focus   **b.** action   **c.** survival

B **Strategy: Summary completion.** Use words and phrases from the passage (including the subheadings) to complete the summary.

There are many dangerous situations, but by working on your

1. _____ skills now, you will be more prepared to face a crisis.

First, stay **2.** _____. You need to believe that you have

3. _____ over what happens to you. If you don't, you'll be less likely

to take **4.** _____. Don't wait for a crisis—work on developing a

postive **5.** _____ now.

Second, focus **6.** _____. If you don't survive, nothing else is important.
Sometimes, you may have to motivate yourself. Yossi Ghinsberg did this by

repeating a(n) **7.** _____ over and over. Once you make sure you

can survive, other things can take **8.** _____ themselves later.
Remembering these skills can mean the difference between life and death.

Language Practice

A Vocabulary: Words in context. Answer the questions below. Share your answers with a partner.

1. When you face a difficult situation do you usually **give up** or keep going?

2. Describe a time when you thought you had a problem, but things **ended up** being OK.

3. If you are **heading** into the rain forest, what are three things you should take?

4. What is the worst **crisis** you have been in?

5. When you are late, do you usually **explain** why?

6. What words would you use to describe your **attitude** toward life?

7. What is a **skill** you would like to learn?

8. Have you ever had a day when everything seemed to **go wrong**? What happened?

B Grammar: Using *when* and *if*. Read the example sentences. Sentence **b** is from the passage.

> **a. When** you find yourself in a crisis, first focus on survival. (The chance this will happen is high.)
>
> **b. If** you find yourself in a crisis, first focus on survival. (This may or may not happen.)

Complete the sentences. Share your answers with a partner.

1. When I see a spider, I _____.

2. If your friend is angry with you, _____.

3. When _____.

4. If _____.

Word Partners

Use *situation* with:
(*adj.*) **bad** situation, **dangerous** situation, **difficult** situation, **political** situation, **terrible** situation, **unique** situation
(*v.*) **describe** a situation, **discuss** a situation, **understand** a situation

▲ Nick Ward on the yacht *Grimalkin* before he is rescued.

Before You Read

A **Discussion.** Look at the picture above and read the information below. What do you think the phrase "left for dead" means?

In his autobiography,[1] *Left for Dead*, Nick Ward writes about being in a yachting race called the Fastnet Race. During the race, the deadliest storm in modern sailing history hit, leaving 15 people dead.

B **Definitions.** Match the words with their meanings.

> **1.** concern   **2.** once   **3.** force (*n.*)   **4.** clear
> **5.** familiar   **6.** spirits   **7.** manage   **8.** goal

_____ **a.** something a person or group is trying to do

_____ **b.** when, as soon as

_____ **c.** something you are worried about

_____ **d.** If someone is this, you have seen them before.

_____ **e.** to be able to do something that is difficult

_____ **f.** power or strength

_____ **g.** without anything in the way; quickly and well

_____ **h.** your feelings, especially happiness or unhappiness

[1] An **autobiography** is a story about someone's life written by the actual person.

Reading

Strategy: Predicting. What survival skills do you think Ward used? Read the passage to check your answers.

☐ a positive attitude
☐ focus on survival
☐ taking action
☐ believing in himself

▲ Nick Ward

Left for Dead

1   For the six people on the *Grimalkin*,
    August 11 seemed like the beginning of
    any other yachting race. But by the night of
    August 13, a powerful storm was throwing the
5   yacht around like a toy.

The next day, one crew member was missing, and Nick and his friend Gerry weren't
moving. Thinking all three were dead, the remaining three sailors left in the small life raft.[1]
Left for dead, and with his friend dying, Nick had to try to survive alone on the yacht.

When I **came to**, nothing looked **familiar**. I was confused. I had to think **clearly**. I could tell
10   the storm was still too strong. But my biggest **concern** was all the water inside the yacht. The
force of one more huge wave, combined with a strong wind, would sink the boat.

Then to my right I saw something blue. A bucket! I reached out for it and fell into the nasty
water. Coughing, I reached out again and **managed** to get the bucket.

For half an hour I kept throwing out buckets of water. It was slow, hard work, but having a
15   purpose and a **goal** lifted my **spirits**. But all too soon I was out of breath and energy. I was
back to worrying, imagining horrible endings. I needed something to keep me **alert**. I started
testing my knowledge. I named lighthouses, then the planets. **Once** I'd finished them, I started
on each planet's moons. Through it all, I kept saying, "I must not fall asleep."

On August 14, three days after the race started, Nick was finally rescued[2] by a helicopter.
20   Gerry had died during those three days, and his body was taken back to his family.

---

[1] A **life raft** is a small boat carried on a larger boat to use in an emergency.
[2] If you **rescue** someone, you save them from a dangerous situation.

Reading Comprehension

A Circle the correct answer.

Detail **1.** How many sailors on the *Grimalkin* survived the race?

    a. two   **b.** three   **c.** four

Paraphrase **2.** In line 9, the phrase **came to** means _____ .

    a. got there   **b.** woke up   **c.** realized it

Detail **3.** At first, throwing water out of the boat made Nick feel _____ .

    a. sick   **b.** tired   **c.** more positive

Vocabulary **4.** In line 16, the word **alert** means _____ .

    a. paying attention   **b.** healthy   **c.** in good spirits

B **Strategy: Labeling a map.** Label the map with the information about the race in the statements below. Write **1–6** on the map.

    1. 303 boats start the race from the Isle of Wight.
    2. 85 boats finish the race.
    3. A helicopter sees the *Grimalkin* and rescues Nick.
    4. An enormous storm heads in from the southwest.
    5. The boats still in the race pass around Fastnet Rock.
    6. The storm hits the *Grimalkin* and the other boats in the race.

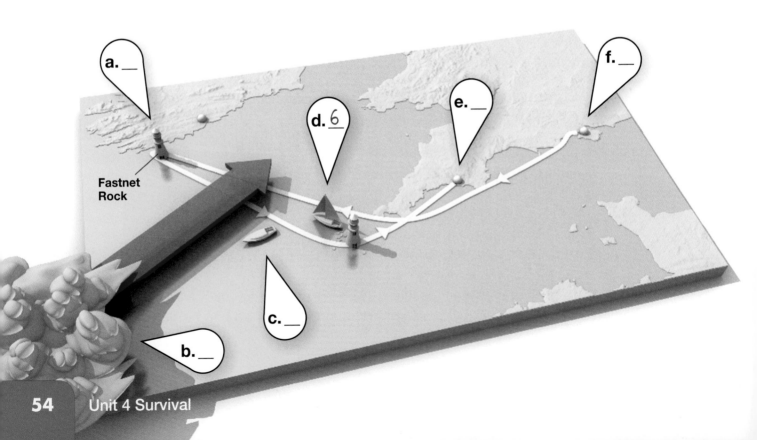

Language Practice

A Vocabulary: Words in context. In each sentence, circle the best answer. The words in **blue** are from the reading.

1. Which of this is more likely to be a **concern** for someone?
   a. their job   **b.** their favorite TV show
2. "**Once** you do your homework" means "_____ your homework."
   a. after you finish   **b.** before you start
3. To measure the **force** of a hurricane, a meteorologist checks the wind's _____.
   a. location   **b.** speed
4. If the answer to a question is **clear**, it is _____ to find.
   a. easy   **b.** difficult
5. You are probably most **familiar** with _____.
   a. a foreign country   **b.** your neighborhood
6. Which of these can lift your **spirits**?
   a. a relaxing holiday   **b.** an elevator
7. When someone **manages** to do something, they do it _____.
   a. with difficulty   **b.** easily
8. Which of these can be a **goal**?
   a. losing weight   **b.** watching TV

Word Partners

Use *familiar* with:
(*prep.*) familiar **with someone/something**
(*n.*) familiar **face**, familiar **to someone**
(*v.*) **look** familiar, **seem** familiar, **sound** familiar, **become** familiar

B Grammar: Passive forms. Read the example sentences. Sentence **b** is from the passage.

   a. People in a helicopter finally **rescued** Nick.

   b. Nick **was** finally **rescued by** a helicopter.

   c. A truck **crushed** Kitts's arm.

   d. Kitts's arm **was crushed by** a truck.

Complete each sentence using the passive form. Compare answers with a partner.

1. My _____ was made in _____.

2. _____ was built in _____.

3. _____ was written by _____.

Survival: Building a Fire

A **Preview.** The words below appear in the video. Match each word with its meaning.

> **1. block**   **2. dry**   **3. novice**   **4. string**

___ **a.** someone who is a beginner at something

___ **b.** a very thin rope

___ **c.** a large rectangular-shaped piece of something

___ **d.** not wet

▲ A Masai man starts a fire using sticks.

B **Watch the video.** Use the words in the box and the picture on the right to explain to a partner how to start a fire using a bow drill. Do you think you would be able to do it?

blow	drill	dry	fuel	hard	hole
knife	string	soft	tight	wood	fire

C **Talk with a partner.** Should people living in cities learn survival skills like starting a fire? Why or why not?

Vocabulary Review

Words in context. Complete each sentence using the words in parentheses.

1. If you _____ that way, you should _____ in town. And once you can _____ some of the buildings, it'll be easy to find your way home. You can't _____! (**end up**, **go wrong**, **head**, **recognize**)

2. The company directors are holding a(n) _____ of interviews this week. They _____ to find someone with the right _____ and _____ to help them reach their _____. (**attitude**, **goals**, **hope**, **series**, **skills**)

3. Researchers have just started to _____ the _____ why some animals can _____ thousands of meters below the _____ of the ocean. (**exist**, **investigate**, **reasons**, **surface**)

4. As the hero faced another _____, his enemies _____ him to _____, but he _____ to keep up his _____ and save the world. (**crisis**, **expected**, **give up**, **managed**, **spirits**)

5. Just before the science fair, our teachers reminded each of us to be as _____ as we could be when we _____ the _____ of our experiment to the judges. They also _____ the importance of speaking slowly and carefully. (**clear**, **emphasized**, **explained**, **process**)

World Heritage Notes

Notes Completion. Scan the information on pages 58 and 59 to complete the notes.

What: SGang Gwaay
Where: British Columbia, Canada
Data:
- The village of SGang Gwaay Llnagaay is on a small beach in the _____ Islands.
- The ruins show us that the _____ people lived here for _____.
- The ruins are made up of hand-built _____ and carved _____.
- The people abandoned the village in _____.
- In 1985, the _____ was created.
- Today, more than _____ Haida live in Canada.

SGang Gwaay

Site: **SGang Gwaay**

Location: **British Columbia, Canada**

Category: **Cultural**

Status: **World Heritage Site since 1981**

Queen
Charlotte
Islands

On a small beach in the Queen Charlotte Islands, a number of tall wooden poles look silently out to sea. They are slowly breaking and some are falling down, but these poles are an important part of the Haida people's history. They are reminders of the wealthy village of SGang Gwaay Ilnagaay, also called Nan Sdins, that stood here.

Here, among the ruins, archeologists have found evidence that the Haida people have lived on these islands for thousands of years. Most of the village is covered by forest, but the ruins that have survived are unique. They show us what a 19th century Haida village looked like, and just how powerful, rich, and beautiful Haida society was at its peak.

Nan Sdins is protected from the ocean wind and waves, and surrounded by thick forests. As a result, the village was not completely destroyed. Visitors today can come and see the large hand-built wooden houses that the Haida lived in, as well as many beautifully carved totem poles.

Each of these totem poles gives us information about the people who carved them, and the people they were carved for. Some stand in front of a house, telling us who lived there. Some tell the myths or legends of the clan. Others were made to remind people of important events in Haida history.

More than 8,000 years ago

The Haida begin to live on the Queen Charlotte Islands.

A.D. 1774

The Spanish ship *Santiago* visits the islands. This is the Haida's first recorded meeting with Europeans.

1788

Englishman Captain George Dixon explores the islands, which are later named after his ship, the *Queen Charlotte*. The Haida begin to trade with the Europeans. However, ships from the outside world also bring diseases that slowly reduce the Haida population to about 300.

1862

A passenger on the *Queen Charlotte* brings the disease smallpox to the island. In less than 20 years, the disease kills most of the Nan Sdins people. There are only about 30 survivors.

1885

The last of the Nan Sdins people abandon the village.

1957

Some of the totem poles from Nan Sdins are moved to museums, so they can be preserved. Many other poles are left at Nan Sdins.

1985

To stop people cutting down trees, and to protect their lands, the Haida people create the "Haida Heritage Site."

Today

The Haida population has grown again. There are more than 4,000 Haida living in Canada. However, fewer than 50 people can speak the Haida language, and many are over 70 years old. The Haida people are working hard to teach the language and culture to Haida children.

How the Raven Stole the Sun

1   In the beginning, the world was completely dark. The Raven was tired of flying around blind and bumping into things.

One day, the Raven found a house by the river, where an old man lived with his daughter. The Raven heard the old man talking about a great treasure—the only light in 5   the world. The man kept the light in a tiny box, which was inside a larger box, which was inside an even larger box, and so on. The Raven decided to steal the light for himself.

First, he tried to find a way into the house. But no matter how hard he looked, he couldn't find a door.

Finally, the Raven came up with a plan. When the old man's daughter came out to get 10   water, he changed himself into a hemlock needle and floated down the river. When the girl took a drink from the river, she swallowed the needle. Once inside the girl, the Raven changed into a very small human and went to sleep.

Then one day, the Raven came out in the shape of a human boy. The old man was surprised at the arrival of his new grandchild, but soon came to love him.

15   Meanwhile, the Raven looked for the light. He found the largest box and carefully opened it, but all he found was another box. The grandfather heard the Ravenchild open the box and scolded him. The Ravenchild asked his grandfather to give him just the largest box to play with.

The old man agreed and gave the Ravenchild the first box. After a while, the Ravenchild 20   demanded that the old man give him the next box. The old man loved his grandson, and agreed. It took many days of crying and begging, but one by one the boxes were removed. When only a few boxes were left, light began to fill the house. Then, the Ravenchild begged his grandfather to let him hold the light for just a moment.

The old man refused at first, but, after a while, he agreed. He took a beautiful, glowing 25   ball of light out of the box and threw it to his grandson. At once, the Raven turned back into a bird, and caught the ball of light in his beak!

Then, moving his powerful wings, he flew through the roof of the house and escaped. Once out of the house, the light spread all over the sky.

And that is how the sun came to be in the sky.

Reading Comprehension

Sequencing. Number the events in the story from **1** (the first) to **8**.

a. _____ Light began to fill the house.

b. _____ The old man gave the light to his grandchild.

c. _____ The old man's daughter swallowed the needle.

d. _____ The Raven found a house.

e. _____ The Raven found the largest box.

f. _____ The Ravenchild appeared.

g. _____ The Sun appeared in the sky.

h. _____ The world was dark.

Vocabulary Extension

Vocabulary: Words for talking about requests. Read the examples. Circle the correct answer to complete each sentence below. Then circle all the request words that appear in the folktale on page 61.

ask	**say something as a question; say you want someone to do something**
	The Ravenchild **asked** his grandfather to give him the largest box to play with.
beg	**ask someone for something in a very serious and emotional way**
	Then, the Ravenchild **begged** his grandfather to let him hold the light for just a moment.
demand	**ask someone for something in a very urgent and forceful way**
	After a while, the Ravenchild **demanded** that the old man give him the next box.

1. The angry crowd (**demanded** / **asked**) that the concert organizers give back their money.

2. He (**begged** / **asked**) us if we went to school today.

3. I (**begged** / **demanded**) my mom to help me with my homework.

4. The whole class (**demanded** / **begged**) our teacher to give us more time to do the test.

5. I was so angry; I (**asked** / **demanded**) that my classmate stop taking my things without asking.

Outer Space

This photo of Earth from the moon was taken by astronauts on the Apollo 8 mission in 1968. They were the first humans to see the entire planet from space.

Warm Up

Talk with a partner.

1. If you could, would you like to go into outer space? Why?

2. Do you think humans will ever start living in outer space? Why or why not?

5A Saturn

Before You Read

▲ Saturn photographed from the *Cassini* spacecraft

A **Quiz.** What do you know about Saturn? Circle True (**T**) or False (**F**) for the sentences below. Then check your answers at the bottom of the page.

1. One of the days of the week was named after Saturn.   **T**   **F**
2. A year on Saturn is more than 29 Earth years.   **T**   **F**
3. A day on Saturn is equal to one Earth month.   **T**   **F**
4. The surface of Saturn is extremely windy.   **T**   **F**
5. Saturn is the biggest planet in our Solar System.   **T**   **F**

B **Definitions.** Match the words with their meanings.

> **1.** mostly   **2.** attract   **3.** major (*adj.*)   **4.** total
>
> **5.** image   **6.** daily   **7.** send   **8.** launch

_____ **a.** important or serious   _____ **e.** when everything is added together

_____ **b.** every day   _____ **f.** picture; idea

_____ **c.** almost all   _____ **g.** to send something into space

_____ **d.** to cause something to go to   _____ **h.** to make people interested in
              another place   something

Answers: 1. T. The day Saturday was named after Saturn. **2.** T **3.** F. A day on Saturn is only 10 hours and 14 minutes. **4.** T **5.** F. It's the second biggest planet in our Solar System, after Jupiter.

Reading

Strategy: Skimming. Read quickly. How large are the rings of Saturn?

THE JEWEL OF THE SOLAR SYSTEM

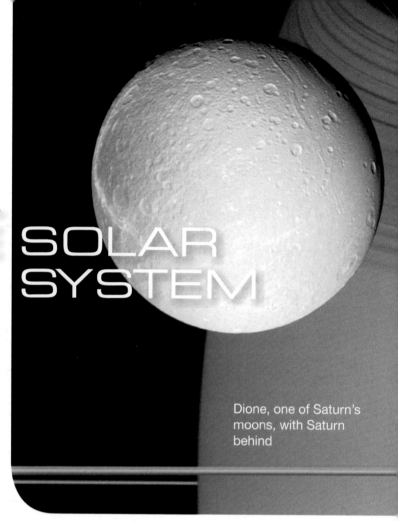

Dione, one of Saturn's moons, with Saturn behind

1 Saturn is huge—more than 700 times the size of Earth. However, it's extremely light—if you could find a big enough ocean to put it in, it would float!

5 That's because Saturn is **mostly** made of gases, including helium, the gas that makes balloons float. But it's the rings around Saturn that give the planet its unique look. And for hundreds of years,

10 it's those rings that people have found so **attractive**.

UNDERSTANDING THE RINGS

At first, Saturn looks like it has just one large ring. However, it actually has seven **major** rings, and each is made up of thousands of smaller ones. In **total**, the rings are more than

15 250,000 kilometers[1] across—that's over two-thirds of the distance from Earth to our moon! **In spite of** this, the rings are quite thin. In fact, on average, they're less than 50 meters[2] thick.

From Earth, the rings look like they are solid, with clear edges. However, this is deceptive.[3] They are actually made from billions of particles[4] of rock and ice. Some particles are as small as a grain of sand. Others are the size of mountains.

20 ## A CLOSER LOOK

Scientists now know a lot about Saturn, but it still holds many mysteries. Because of this, 17 countries worked together to build a spacecraft, called *Cassini*. **Launched** in October 1997, *Cassini* started **sending** information from Saturn to Earth in 2004. Its **images** and videos have been extremely valuable. For example, in 2008, scientists found evidence that

25 one of Saturn's moons might contain basic life forms.[5]

All these years later, *Cassini* still sends **daily** information back to Earth. Using this data, scientists will continue to make exciting new discoveries for many years to come.

[1] 250,000 kilometers = 155,000 miles
[2] 50 meters = 165 feet
[3] If something is **deceptive**, it makes you believe something that is not true.
[4] A **particle** of something is a very small piece of it.
[5] A **life form** is any living thing, such as an animal or plant.

Reading Comprehension

A Circle the correct answer.

Detail   **1.** According to the passage, which sentence about Saturn is true?

      a. Saturn has large oceans, just like Earth.
      b. Saturn has 700 moons.
      c. One of the things that makes up Saturn is helium.

Detail   **2.** In total, Saturn has _____ ring(s).

      a. one   **b.** seven   **c.** thousands of

Paraphrase   **3.** In line 16, the phrase **in spite of** has a similar meaning to _____ .

      a. in addition   **b.** although   **c.** therefore

Detail   **4.** Which of these is NOT an example of the data that *Cassini* sends back to Earth?

      a. pictures   **b.** information   **c.** life forms

B **Strategy: Identifying true, false, or not given.** Are these sentences about the passage true (**T**), false (**F**), or is the information not given in the passage (**NG**)?

1. The Earth is bigger than Saturn.	**T**	**F**	**NG**
2. For many generations, people have been interested in Saturn's rings.	**T**	**F**	**NG**
3. It is more than 250,000 kilometers from Earth to Earth's moon.	**T**	**F**	**NG**
4. The reason why many countries worked together to build *Cassini* is because it was so expensive.	**T**	**F**	**NG**
5. Some of the videos from *Cassini* show life forms.	**T**	**F**	**NG**
6. *Cassini* sends data to Earth once a week.	**T**	**F**	**NG**

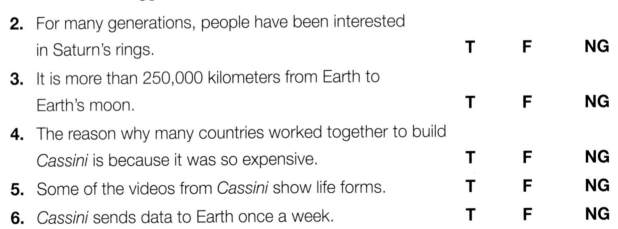

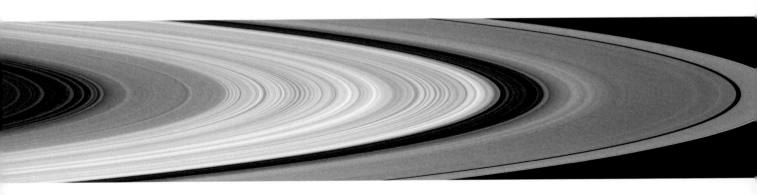

▲ Saturn's rings are made from billions of particles of rock and ice.

Language Practice

A **Vocabulary: Words in context.** Complete the sentences. Share your answers with a partner.

1. On the weekends, I **mostly** _____.

2. _____ is one of my country's **major** festivals.

3. Watching a rocket being **launched** sounds _____.

4. **In total** there are _____.

5. I probably see about _____ **images** in a typical day.

6. An example of something I do **daily** is _____.

7. I **send** (more / fewer) SMS texts than I receive—about _____ a week.

8. A popular tourist spot in my country is _____. Tourists are mainly **attracted** to it by _____.

B **Grammar: Passive forms.** Read the example sentences from the passage.

> **a.** . . . each **is made up of** thousands of smaller ones.
>
> **b.** That's because Saturn **is** mostly **made of** gases.
>
> **c.** They **are** actually **made from** billions of particles of rock and ice.

Rewrite each of the sentences using the passive form.

1. Two hydrogen atoms and one oxygen atom make water.

   Water _____.

2. Cooling magma that released water vapor made the oceans.

   The oceans _____.

3. Oceans cover most of the Earth's surface.

   Most _____.

4. Plants create most of Earth's oxygen.

   _____.

Word Partners

Use *total* with:
(*adj.*) **grand** total
(*n.*) total **cost**, total **expenses**, total **sales**, total **savings**, total **value**, total **area**

5B To the Moon

Before You Read

▲ American astronaut Edwin "Buzz" Aldrin stands on the moon.

A **Quiz.** What do you know about trips to the moon? Circle True (**T**) or False (**F**) for the sentences below. Then check your answers at the bottom of the page.

1.	NASA was created in the 1980s.	**T**	**F**
2.	The first living being to go into space was a human.	**T**	**F**
3.	A Russian—Yuri Gagarin—was the first person in space.	**T**	**F**
4.	The first people to walk on the moon were Neil Armstrong and Edwin Aldrin.	**T**	**F**
5.	No one has been to the moon since 1972.	**T**	**F**

B **Definitions.** Match the words with their meanings.

> **1.** put off **2.** decade **3.** willing **4.** mission
> **5.** president **6.** stand (*v.*) **7.** stress **8.** equipment

_____ **a.** a period of ten years

_____ **b.** an important job, usually requiring travel

_____ **c.** difficulties and problems

_____ **d.** to do something later than planned

_____ **e.** the leader of a company or country

_____ **f.** to experience something difficult without being harmed

_____ **g.** agreeing to do something

_____ **h.** the things you need (e.g., machines) to do something

Answers: 1. F. It was started in the 1950s. **2.** F. The Russians sent a dog named Laika in 1957. **3.** T. He went into space on April 12, 1961. **4.** T **5.** T

Reading

Strategy: Skimming.
Quickly read the speech below. What is the main topic President Kennedy talked about?

_____

_____

President John F. Kennedy ▶
speaking in Texas, 1962

We choose to go to the moon.

1   *The following is adapted from a speech United States **President** John F. Kennedy gave in Houston, Texas, on September 12, 1962.*

Why, some say, the moon? Why choose this as our goal? And they may ask: why climb the highest mountain? Why, 35 years ago, fly
5   across the Atlantic?

We choose to go to the moon. We choose to go to the moon in this **decade**, not because it is easy, but because it is hard. But the challenge is one that we are **willing** to accept. It is one we are unwilling to **put off**.

10   To send a rocket to the moon, we must be bold.[1] The moon is 240,000 miles away[2] from the Earth. And the rocket is just 300 feet[3] tall. The rocket will need new kinds of metal, some of which have not yet been invented. It must be able to **stand** heat and **stresses** like those never experienced before. It will need to carry all the **equipment** it needs—all on an untried **mission**, to an unknown place. And
15   then it must return safely to Earth by re-entering the atmosphere at speeds of over 25,000 miles[4] per hour, causing heat about half that of the temperature of the sun. We want to do all this. And we want to do it right. And do it first, before this decade is out!

Many years ago, the great British explorer George Mallory, who died on Mount Everest, was asked why he wanted to climb it. He said, "Because it is there."

20   Well, space is there, and we're going to climb it. The moon and the planets are there. New hopes for knowledge and peace are there. And, therefore, we start on **the most dangerous and greatest adventure** that man has ever tried.

[1] Someone who is **bold** is not afraid to do dangerous things.   [3] 300 feet = 90 meters
[2] 240,000 miles = 386,000 kilometers   [4] 25,000 miles = 40,000 kilometers

Reading Comprehension

A Circle the correct answer.

Purpose **1.** What was President Kennedy's main purpose in this speech?

    a. to explain why the trip to the moon would be expensive
    b. to make the people of the United States excited about the mission
    c. to make people consider becoming rocket scientists

Detail **2.** Which part of the mission does President Kennedy say is particularly difficult?

    a. the launch   **b.** leaving the moon   **c.** the re-entry to Earth

Paraphrase **3.** What did Mallory mean when he said "Because it is there" (line 19)?

    a. Being the first to do something is a good reason to do it.
    b. It was his job to climb Mt. Everest.
    c. He needed to prove the location of Mt. Everest.

Inference **4.** President Kennedy suggested the real reason to go to the moon is _____.

    a. to make money   **b.** to study the moon   **c.** to prove it is possible

B **Strategy: Notes completion.**
Complete the notes with words
from the reading.

Going to the moon

Challenges

1. The moon is _____ kilometers from Earth.

2. need to invent new kinds of _____

3. need to carry a lot of _____

4. do it before the end of the _____

Dangers

5. re-entry at very high _____—over 40,000 kilometers/hour

6. rocket must face terrible heat and _____

7. temperatures are almost half that of _____

Language Practice

A Vocabulary: Completion. Complete the sentences using the words in the box.

> decade   stress   put off   willing
>
> mission   stand   president   equipment

1. If it rains, we'll _____ the picnic until next week.
2. The Roaring Twenties is used to talk about the _____ between 1920 and 1929.
3. Firefighters must be _____ to go into dangerous situations.
4. The Space Shuttle's last _____ was in 2011.
5. Every four years Americans choose their _____.
6. Most people can't _____ loud noise when they are trying to work.
7. Doctors say that too much _____ is bad for a person's health.
8. A bat and baseball are examples of sports _____.

B Grammar: *Going to* and *will*. Read the example sentences. Sentence **a** is from the passage.

> **a.** Well, space is there, and we**'re going to** climb it.
>
> **b.** I**'ll** call you later on, I**'m going to** study first.

Complete the sentences below, using *will* or *going to*. Circle the correct answers.

1. I'm so tired. When I get home, (**I'll** / **I'm going to**) sit down and relax.
2. I'm busy after school; (**I'll** / **I'm going to**) visit my grandparents.
3. I'm doing something at the moment. (**I'll** / **I'm going to**) help you later.
4. There's too much to study for the test. (**I'll** / **I'm going to**) never remember everything.

> ## Word Partners
>
> Use *mission* with:
> (adj.) **dangerous** mission, **secret** mission, **successful** mission
> (n.) **rescue** mission, **training** mission
> (v.) **accomplish** a mission, **carry out** a mission, **complete** a mission

The first launch of the Saturn 5 rocket that later carried three astronauts to the moon. ▼

▲ The crew of Apollo 11, the first mission to the moon. From left: Neil Armstrong, Michael Collins, and Edwin "Buzz" Aldrin

A **Preview.** You will hear these words in the video. Match each word to its definition.

> **a.** astronaut **b.** crew **c.** courage
> **d.** leap **e.** mankind **f.** universe

___ **1.** all humans

___ **2.** the whole of space and all the stars, planets, etc. in it

___ **3.** a jump, a large and important increase

___ **4.** the willingness to do something dangerous despite your fear

___ **5.** the people who work on a ship, plane, or spaceship

___ **6.** a person who goes into outer space

B **After you watch.** Number the events in the correct order, **1–6**.

___ **a.** Americans send Alan Shepard into space.

___ **b.** Apollo 11 lands people on the moon.

___ **c.** John Glenn goes around the Earth three times.

___ **d.** The Soviet Union sends a person into space.

___ **e.** The Soviet Union launch Sputnik.

___ **f.** Russian and American astronauts work together on the International Space Station.

C **Think about it.** On the moon, Neil Armstrong said, "That's one small step for man. One giant leap for mankind." What do you think he meant? Discuss with a partner.

A copy of the Rosetta Stone. The original stone is over 2,000 years old, and was discovered in Egypt in 1799. The stone contains the same text in three languages, and allowed people to translate Egyptian hieroglyphics.

Warm Up

Talk with a partner.

1. Do you prefer to talk to someone or send an email or text message? Why?

2. How do you think the world would be different without writing?

6A | Writing around the World

Before You Read

A **Discussion.** Look at the pictures. Which kinds of writings have you seen before? Where? What do you know about the history of writing?

B **Definitions.** Match the words with their meanings.

> **1.** represent   **2.** various   **3.** relationship   **4.** character
> **5.** perhaps   **6.** press   **7.** influence (*n.*)   **8.** count (*v.*)

_____ **a.** maybe

_____ **b.** to find the number of something

_____ **c.** the power to have an effect on something

_____ **d.** to mean something; to be an example of something

_____ **e.** many different

_____ **f.** to push something hard

_____ **g.** the way two things or people behave toward each other

_____ **h.** a sign; something like a letter in some languages

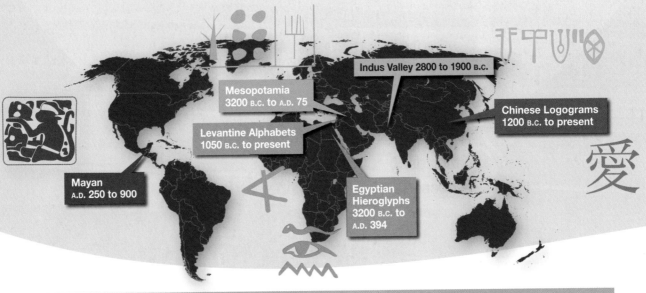

Indus Valley 2800 to 1900 B.C.

Mesopotamia 3200 B.C. to A.D. 75

Chinese Logograms 1200 B.C. to present

Levantine Alphabets 1050 B.C. to present

Mayan A.D. 250 to 900

Egyptian Hieroglyphs 3200 B.C. to A.D. 394

Mesopotamia 3200 B.C. to A.D. 75
Egyptian Hieroglyphs 3200 B.C. to A.D. 394
Indus Valley 2800 to 1900 B.C.
Chinese Logograms 1200 B.C. to present
Levantine Alphabets 1050 B.C. to present
Mayan A.D. 2

| **3000** B.C. | **2000** | **1000**

Reading

Strategy: Predicting.
Which culture do you think
first invented writing?

FIVE THOUSAND YEARS OF WRITING

1   No other invention—except **perhaps** the wheel—has had a longer and greater impact on human culture than writing. In fact, the history and culture of many **civilizations** is only measured from the point that they developed writing.

The Sumerians first started to record[1] the numbers of objects they **counted** by **pressing** reeds
5   into wet clay. Since then, humans have been looking for the perfect tool to record their ideas.

The earliest forms of writing were pictographic—in other words, pictures were used to **represent** objects. Chinese writing is an example of this. Originally, the **characters** looked like pictures. However, over the centuries, they became less picture-like and faster to write. Another example of pictographic writing is ancient Mayan. The Maya used pictures to
10   write dates. For example, in one character, a monkey holds a head over a skull. The monkey represents a day, and the head stands for the number six. Since the skull stands for ten, together, the pictogram represents 16 days. **Interestingly**, of the **various** cultures that used pictographic writing, only Chinese is widespread today.

As writing developed, the **relationship** between characters and the objects they represented
15   became less strong. Writing became phonetic—letters represented sounds, like in the modern English alphabet. The phonetic alphabet developed by the Phoenicians about 3,000 years ago **influenced** the writing of modern Hebrew, Arabic, Greek, and English.

Today, about 85 percent of the world's population can read and write. Whatever form of writing those people use, it remains one of humanity's most powerful forms of artistic and
20   creative expression.

[1] If you **record** something, you write it down or take a picture of it, so you can remember it in the future.

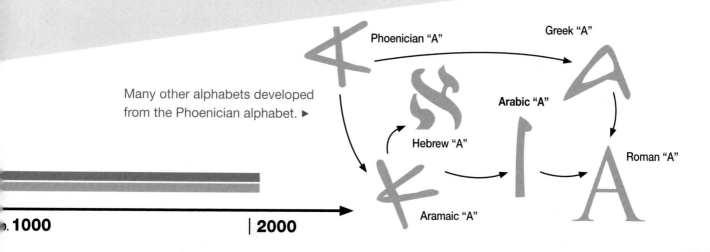

Many other alphabets developed from the Phoenician alphabet. ▶

Phoenician "A"   Greek "A"
Arabic "A"
Hebrew "A"   Roman "A"
Aramaic "A"

1000 | 2000

Reading Comprehension

A Circle the correct answer.

Vocabulary **1.** Which word is closest in meaning to **civilizations** (line 2).

    a. languages   **b.** societies   **c.** generations

Inference **2.** Why does the writer use **interestingly** in line 12?

    a. to show it is surprising that pictographs were once common but now rare
    b. because Chinese once used a phonetic alphabet
    c. to explain that pictographic writing systems are easier to learn and use

Detail **3.** Writing developed because people needed a way to _____.

    a. remember their ideas
    b. influence future generations
    c. continue their human relationships

Detail **4.** According to the passage, what percentage of people in the world today cannot read or write?

    a. 5 percent   **b.** 15 percent   **c.** 85 percent

B **Strategy: Classification.**
Match each description (**a–f**)
with the correct writing system.

    a. a phonetic system
    b. a pictographic system
    c. pictographic characters
    became less like
    pictures
    d. still in use today
    e. used to record and
    share information
    f. shares an ancestor
    with Arabic and
    Hebrew

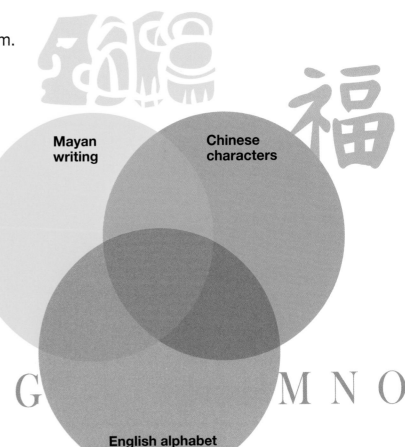

Mayan writing

Chinese characters

English alphabet

A B C D E F G ... M N O

Language Practice

A **Vocabulary: Words in context.** In each sentence, circle the best answer. The words in **blue** are from the reading.

1. Which of these **represents** a sound in English _____?
   a. a pronunciation symbol, such as ð   **b.** a video interview with someone

2. Most people have **various** kinds of _____.
   a. accents   **b.** clothes

3. Which of these people have a closer **relationship**?
   a. a driver and a passenger   **b.** a granddaughter and grandfather

4. Which of these is a **character**?
   a. 愛   **b.** "cat"

5. If you say **perhaps**, you are _____.
   a. certain   **b.** not sure

6. Which of these do you usually **press**?
   a. a button   **b.** a rope

7. Is it possible that modern English **influenced** the old Phoenician alphabet?
   a. Yes.   **b.** No.

8. Which of these can you **count**?
   a. hamburgers   **b.** honey

B **Grammar: Using *in other words*.** Read the example sentences. Sentence **a** is from the passage.

a. The earliest forms of writing were pictographic—**in other words**, pictures were used to represent objects.

b. Saturn could contain more than 700 Earths. **In other words**, it is huge.

Word Partners

Use *influence* with:
(*adj.*) **important** influence, **major** influence, **powerful** influence, **strong** influence, **bad/good** influence
(*n.*) influence **opinion**, influence **people**
(*v.*) **have an** influence **on someone**

Complete the sentence below. Then write two more sentences.

1. The Sumerians started to develop their writing system in 3,200 B.C. Mayans started using picture characters in about A.D. 250. In other words, _____

   _____.

2. _____

   _____.

3. _____

   _____.

6B Why Do People Read?

Before You Read

A **Discussion.** Do you like reading? Why do you think most people read? Do you think people living 100 years ago read more or less than people living today? Talk about your ideas with a partner.

B **Definitions.** Match the words with their meanings.

> **1.** stay up **2.** pleasure **3.** education **4.** gain (*v.*)
> **5.** personal **6.** word of mouth **7.** necessary **8.** physical

_____ **a.** the process of learning in schools

_____ **b.** able to be seen and touched

_____ **c.** to not go to bed, even though it's late

_____ **d.** something you must have or do is ____

_____ **e.** passing information through speaking

_____ **f.** to get something

_____ **g.** about you or a certain person

_____ **h.** a feeling of enjoyment

Reading

Strategy: Skimming. In the essay below, the writer lists three ways books are used. Which of these does he NOT talk about?

a. for fun   **c.** for inspiration

b. for religious reasons   **d.** for information

The Companionship¹ of Books

▲ Arthur Elmore Bostwick (1860–1942) was an American librarian and president of the American Library Association.

1   *This essay is adapted from "The Companionship of Books," first published in* A Librarian's Open Shelf *(1920).*

Are books our companions? That depends. You and I read them with **pleasure**; others do not care for them. To some, the reading of any book is as impossible as reading a
5 book in a foreign language. These people do not read—at all. Take a New York police officer. Someone suggested he ought to read a novel in his **vacation²** time, but he said, "Well, I've never read a book yet, and I don't think I'll begin now." He had no use for books. He could get along perfectly well without³ them, and he is not unique. **These people** are not **uneducated**; they have and are still **gaining** much knowledge. However,
10 they gain this knowledge not from books, but by **personal** experience and by **word of mouth**. Is it possible that they are right? Could it be true that reading books is not **necessary**?

To answer these questions, let's stop and think about books. Books may be used in three ways. First, a book can give us information. It is valuable not because it a **physical**
15 object, made of paper and ink, but because it records ideas that can pass from generation to generation. Second, reading can be fun. When a reader loves an exciting story and cannot stop reading, he **stays up** late at night reading. Finally, books can inspire. Reading about how to make a box may inspire a boy to go out and make one himself. And inspiration goes beyond boxes! A good idea in a book can make those who read it
20 into better men or women.

What do all these examples show us? Books make it possible for ideas to go beyond one person, to cross places and time. This is **the miracle⁴ of writing**—a miracle that is repeated daily in millions of places with millions of readers.

---

¹ **Companionship** is being with someone you know and like.
² A **vacation** is a period of time when you are away from work or school.
³ If you can **get along without** something, you don't need it.
⁴ A **miracle** is a good event that is surprising and unexpected.

Reading Comprehension

A Circle the correct answer.

Inference **1.** The author of the essay _____ the police officer's opinion.

    a. can't explain   **b.** disagrees with   **c.** agrees with

Reference **2.** In lines 8–9, **these people** refers to people who _____.

    a. think everyone should read
    b. believe they don't need to read
    c. are getting information by reading

Detail **3.** According to the author, books are important because of _____.

    a. who wrote them
    b. when they were written
    c. what is in them

Inference **4.** According to the author, **the miracle of writing** (line 22) is the _____.

    a. inspiration of others
    b. joy of reading
    c. sharing of thoughts across time

B **Strategy: Identifying fact and opinion.** Which of these statements about reading are facts (**F**), and which are opinions (**O**)? With a partner, talk about which opinions you agree with and why.

_____ **a.** Without books, you cannot gain knowledge.

_____ **b.** Books make it possible for us to know what happened hundreds of years ago.

_____ **c.** Writing is a miracle.

_____ **d.** Millions of people read each day.

_____ **e.** The New York police officer ought to read so he can be better educated.

_____ **f.** Reading always inspires people.

Language Practice

A **Vocabulary: Words in context.** Answer the questions below. Share your answers with a partner.

1. When was the last time you **stayed up** all night?

2. Name something that gives you **pleasure**.

3. How many years of **education** have you had?

4. What can you do to **gain** experience with different cultures?

5. Which is more important: **personal** experience or knowledge from books?

6. What is one thing you have learned through **word of mouth**?

7. Do you think books are **necessary**, now that we have the Internet?

8. Which do you prefer: **physical** books or electronic books? Why?

B **Grammar: Using *ought to*.** Read the example sentences. Sentence **a** is from the passage.

a. Someone suggested he **ought to** read a novel in his vacation time.

b. If you are heading into the rain forest, what are three things you **ought to** take?

Complete the sentences with **ought to** and your ideas. Compare answers with a partner.

1. I ought to _____.

2. Teachers often say, "_____."

3. _____.

4. _____.

Word Partners

Use *physical* with:
(*n.*) physical **education**, physical **activity**, physical **fitness**,
physical **health**, physical **condition**, physical **environment**,
physical **examination**, physical **strength**

Where Writing Began

◄ cuneiform
writing

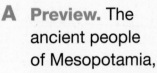

A **Preview.** The ancient people of Mesopotamia, in what is now Iraq, used a form of writing called cuneiform, in which pictures represent physical objects. Look at the cuneiform characters below. What thing do you think each character represents?

1.  _____   3. _____

2. _____   4. _____

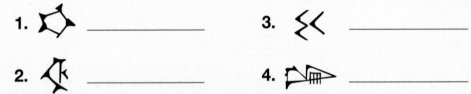

B **After you watch.** Watch the video. Then match each of the names in the left column with its description.

1. Babylon   ○   ○ **a.** a king who wanted to live forever

2. cuneiform   ○   ○ **b.** a king who wrote a set of laws

3. Gilgamesh   ○   ○ **c.** a kingdom famous for its hanging gardens

4. Hammurabi   ○   ○ **d.** an ancient city

5. Mesopotamia ○   ○ **e.** an ancient civilization who developed writing

6. Nineveh   ○   ○ **f.** an area in what is now Iraq

7. Sumerians   ○   ○ **g.** a form of writing

C **Think about it.** How would we know about the past if writing had not been invented?

Vocabulary Review

Crossword. Complete the crossword puzzle with words from Units 5 and 6.

Across

3. almost full
5. maybe
6. to find how many of something there is
8. ten years
9. to be an example of something
15. make people interested in something

17. move something to another place
18. to have an effect on something
19. ready and happy to do something

Down

1. push against something
2. experience something without being harmed
3. an important job
4. send a rocket up into the air
7. related only to you, belonging to you
10. the process of learning, building knowledge

11. able to be seen or touched
12. to get more of something
13. do something later
14. picture
16. the whole amount

World Heritage Notes

Notes Completion. Scan the information on pages 84 and 85 to complete the notes.

What: The Bend of the Boyne   Where: County Meath, Ireland
Data:

• There are three great _____ at the Bend of the Boyne. One is called Newgrange.

• Newgrange is more than _____ years old.

• Some scientists think it was built by a small community of _____, others think it was built by a large organized _____.

• According to Irish legends, Newgrange was once _____ of the Irish god-kings.

• Newgrange also has an amazing secret. At _____ on the winter solstice (_____ day of the year), the sun shines in and lights up the corridor.

The Bend of the Boyne

Site: **The Bend of the Boyne**

Location: **County Meath, Ireland**

Category: **Cultural**

Status: **World Heritage Site since 1993**

Ireland

For more than 5,000 years, this huge round structure, called Newgrange, has stood by Ireland's River Boyne. Today, Newgrange is one of three great burial mounds which make up the World Heritage Site known as the Bend of the Boyne.

Some historians think that it was once the center of a small, simple community of farmers. Others, considering the techniques and tools that might be required to build it, believe it was built by a more advanced society. Newgrange itself gives few clues. As a result, it is still very much a mystery to both visitors and experts. One of the things we do know, however, is that it took many years to build. This means it was an important enough project to pass from one generation to the next.

Inside the mound is a long tunnel made of huge stones, many with beautiful carvings of ancient Celtic symbols. At the end of tunnel— at the center of the structure—is a room where a stone basin held the ashes and bones of the ancient dead.

This suggests Newgrange was a tomb, but many believe it was more. For example, legends of the area speak of it being the palace of god-kings. Whether it was built as a tomb by a small group of farmers, or as a palace by a large, organized tribe, Newgrange stands today as an amazing example of the efforts and art of ancient people.

For many years since its discovery, people thought Newgrange was just a tomb. However, in the late 1960s, archeologists uncovered an amazing secret that happens every year on the shortest day of the year. At dawn on that day—the winter solstice—as sunlight hits the building, the sun enters a window above the main entrance. The sunlight lights up the entire 20-meter corridor that leads to the basin of ancestral bones.

This special feature is not only an impressive feat of engineering for its ancient builders. It also tell us Newgrange was probably also an important place of worship, a place for people to gather to honor their ancestors.

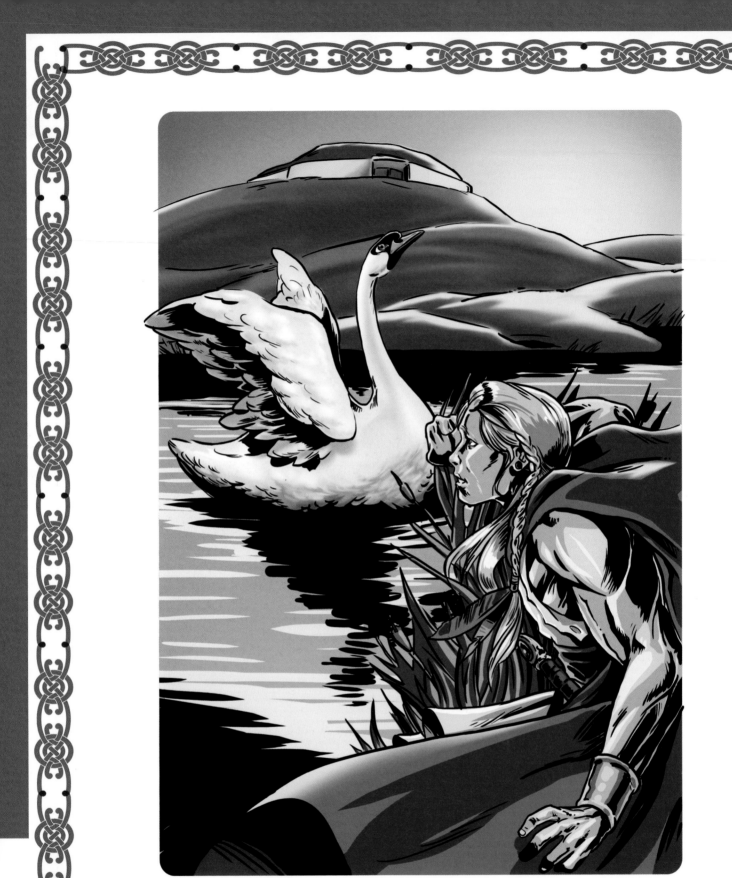

AN IRISH FOLKTALE
AONGHUS
AND CAER

1 Once upon a time, at Newgrange, there lived a young god named Aonghus. One night, a beautiful girl visited Aonghus in a dream. But when he put out his arms to touch her, she disappeared. The next day, Aonghus was so sad he wouldn't eat anything.

5 That night, the girl appeared in his dreams again. This time, she played beautiful music and sang to him. But once again, she disappeared.

Aonghus fell in love with the girl in his dreams. But he could not be with her. For a whole year, Aonghus would not eat, and he grew thinner and sicker.

His friends and family searched for this mysterious girl. Finally, they found
10 her, surrounded by one hundred and fifty other girls, who were tied together **in pairs** by silver chains. Her name was Caer, and she was the daughter of the fairy king.

Immediately, Aonghus went to ask Caer's father to let him marry her. But Caer's father told Aonghus that he had no power over her, and that she had gone to
15 a lake where she would turn into a swan and live in her swan-form for a year. However, if he could identify Caer in her swan-form, she might agree to marry him.

When Aonghus found the lake, there were many beautiful swans on it. They all looked so similar. Aonghus heard a song coming from across the lake. It
20 was the song Caer had sung in his dreams. He called to her and asked her to marry him. Caer agreed, but only if he too would become a swan for a while. He agreed, and changed into a swan. Together, they flew three times around the lake, and then flew to Newgrange, where after some time they turned back into humans and lived happily ever after.

Reading Comprehension

Circle the correct answer.

1. What did Aonghus see in his dreams?

   a. a swan   **b.** a girl   **c.** a lake

2. In line 11, **in pairs** means _____.

   a. in groups of two   **b.** in small groups   **c.** all the girls together

3. At the lake, Aonghus saw _____.

   a. beautiful swans   **b.** a hundred and fifty girls   **c.** his family and friends

4. How did Aonghus know which swan was Caer?

   a. she was the most beautiful swan   **b.** he heard her singing   **c.** the fairy king told him

5. What did Caer want Aonghus to do?

   a. fly to Newgrange   **b.** turn her into a human   **c.** become a swan

Language Extension

Grammar: Reported Speech. Look at the examples. Then change the direct speech to reported speech in the statements below.

Aonghus's friends: "Her name **is** Caer, and she **is** the daughter of the fairy king."

Aonghus' friends **said that** her name **was** Caer, and that she **was** the daughter of the fairy king.

Aonghus's friends and family: "We **found** the girl."

They **said that** they **had found** the girl.

1. "I finished my homework."
   He said that _____.

2. "My brother's not at home."
   She said that _____.

3. "She left the classroom."
   They said that _____.

4. "I'm sorry."
   He said that _____.

5. "I live in Ireland."
   He said that _____.

Alice and the
White Rabbit in a
theater production of
Alice in Wonderland

Warm Up

Talk with a partner.

1. What was your favorite book when you were young? Why did you like it?

2. Who are some of your favorite authors now? Why do you like them?

The Wonderland of Lewis Carroll

▲ This drawing shows scenes from *Alice in Wonderland*.

Before You Read

A **Discussion.** What do you know about the story *Alice in Wonderland*? If you don't know it, look at the illustration above, and guess what happens. Tell a partner.

B **Definitions.** Match the words with their meanings.

> **1.** boring   **2.** character   **3.** complain   **4.** in particular
> **5.** offer   **6.** role   **7.** shy   **8.** social

_____ **a.** a job; the things a person has to do

_____ **b.** especially

_____ **c.** feeling uncomfortable with new people

_____ **d.** a person in a story (e.g., a movie or book)

_____ **e.** relating to other people

_____ **f.** not interesting

_____ **g.** to say that you are willing to do something

_____ **h.** to say that you don't like something

▲ Lewis Carroll is the name Charles Lutwidge Dodgson (1832–1898) used when writing his books.

Reading

Strategy: Scanning.
Dodgson said, "The three little girls were in the garden most of the time, and we became excellent friends." Quickly read the passage and write the names of the girls.

1. _____
2. _____
3. _____

▲ A copy of the *Alice in Wonderland* manuscript and a photo of Alice sit in front of a window in Dodgson's room.

The Beginning of

1 Many people described Charles Lutwidge Dodgson as **shy**. He wasn't very good in **social** situations. One of his college students even said Dodgson's math classes were extremely **boring**. Children, however, thought very differently of him. When he was with children, he was funny and imaginative. He invented puzzles and games, and created stories that children
5 loved. Those children included Alice Pleasance Liddell, the daughter of a colleague, and her two sisters, Lorina and Edith. Dodgson was, it seems, a wildflower that only bloomed¹ when children were around.

"Tell us a story, please, Mr. Dodgson," the three girls asked.

"Alice was beginning to get very tired of sitting by her sister on the side of the river and of
10 having nothing to do. Suddenly, a white rabbit with pink eyes ran close by her," he began. He continued for a few minutes, and then stopped. "That's all until next time."

The girls **complained**, so he **offered** to go on. That day the stories came out one after another. He seemed relaxed in his **role** as storyteller. Dodgson included the children in the stories, with Alice as the most important **character**. The other characters included an Eaglet (named for
15 Edith) and a Lory (a kind of parrot) named after Lorina. That day, **in particular**, Dodgson's stories were really interesting.

Later, Alice begged² Dodgson to write the stories down, and he agreed. However, it wasn't until two and a half years later that Dodgson finally gave her a dark green leather³ notebook, the beginning of the stories we now know as *Alice's Adventures in Wonderland*.

---

¹ When a flower **blooms**, it opens.
² If you **beg** someone to do something, you ask them again and again.
³ **Leather** is the skin of a cow, used for making clothes, shoes, etc.

Reading Comprehension

A Circle the correct answer.

Inference **1.** According to the passage, in which of these situations would Dodgson probably have felt most comfortable?

a. at a party   **b.** teaching a class   **c.** at a picnic with children

Paraphrase **2.** In line 6, the author probably compared Dodgson to a wildflower to show that he was _____.

a. only really relaxed with children
b. difficult to really understand
c. inventive and very imaginative

Detail **3.** The "Lory" was based on _____.

a. Alice's sister   **b.** an eagle   **c.** a character in Dodgson's book

Detail **4.** Which of these statements about *Alice's Adventures in Wonderland* is NOT true?

a. It was originally written for children.
b. Alice Liddell wrote some of the stories in the book.
c. Some of the characters were based on people Dodgson knew.

B Strategy: Identifying main and supporting ideas. Are the statements below main ideas (M) or supporting ideas (S)? Write M or S next to each idea.

_____ **a.** Dodgson was popular with children.

_____ **b.** Some students thought Dodgson's math classes were boring.

_____ **c.** Many people thought Dodgson wasn't good in social situations.

_____ **d.** Dodgson invented puzzles.

_____ **e.** Dodgson was very creative.

_____ **f.** The children listened, very interested in what happened to the rabbit.

Dodgson wasn't afraid to tease himself. ▶ This drawing of his shows "what I look like when I'm [teaching]."

Language Practice

A Vocabulary: Completion. Complete the sentences using the words in the box.

> social   offers   boring   shy
> particularly character   complained   role

1. Dodgson's math students _____ about his classes, saying they were not interesting.
2. Many people think books written 100 years ago are _____.
3. Alice is the main _____ in *Alice's Adventures in Wonderland*.
4. At a new job, it can sometimes take time for someone to feel comfortable in their new _____.
5. Charles Dodgson appeared _____ with people he didn't know well. He didn't seem relaxed when he was with them.
6. In *Alice's Adventures in Wonderland*, a caterpillar _____ Alice a mushroom that can help her get bigger or smaller.
7. When something is _____ good, you can say it is "amazing."
8. A wedding is an example of a(n) _____ event.

B Grammar: Using *tired of*. Read the example sentences. Sentence **A** is from the passage.

> **a.** Alice was beginning to get very **tired of** sitting by her sister on the side of the river.
>
> **b.** I'm **tired of** studying. I've been in the library for hours.

Complete these sentences. Compare your answers with a partner.

1. It's easy to get tired of people who _____ all the time.
2. I don't think I'll ever get tired of _____.
3. My _____ said _____ tired of _____.
4. I'm tired of _____.

Word Partners

Use *role* with:
(*adj.*) **important** role, **major** role, **traditional** role, **bigger** role, **active** role, **starring** role; (*n.*) lead **role**, leadership **role**; (*v.*) **play** a role, **take** on a role

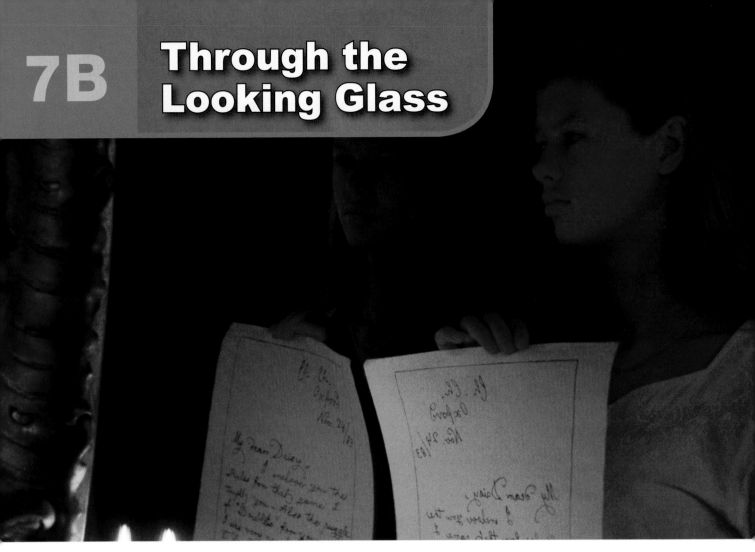

Before You Read

▲ Looking glasses (mirrors) are a regular feature of Dodgson's writings for children. In this picture, a letter from Dodgson uses mirror writing to keep its message secret.

A Discussion. Dodgson loved to make games and puzzles, like the mirror writing above. Do you like games or puzzles? If so, what kind? Tell a partner.

B Definitions. Match the words with their meanings.

> **1.** evening   **2.** fade   **3.** golden   **4.** memory
>
> **5.** pleased   **6.** eager   **7.** publish   **8.** simple

_____ **a.** the time between the end of the afternoon and the time you go to bed

_____ **b.** to become weaker; to slowly disappear

_____ **c.** easy to understand; not having many parts

_____ **d.** happy

_____ **e.** to make a book, magazine, etc.

_____ **f.** having a deep yellow color

_____ **g.** wanting to do or have something very much

_____ **h.** something from the past that you remember

Reading

Strategy: Scanning. Dodgson hid a secret message in the poem below. What is it? _____

A Boat Beneath a Sunny Sky

1 In *Alice's Adventures in Wonderland*,
Alice falls into a rabbit hole and explores
the wonderland that Dodgson created. In
real life, the stories started one day while
5 Dodgson was in a rowboat on a small
lake with some friends, including three
little girls. Many years after creating the
first stories about Alice, Dodgson wrote
that he could recall that day, "almost as
10 clearly as if it were yesterday."

Six years after *Alice's Adventures in
Wonderland*, Dodgson **published**
another book, *Through the Looking Glass*,
which continues the Alice stories. He
15 included his **memories** of that day on the
lake in this untitled poem at the end of
Through the Looking Glass.

A boat, beneath¹ a sunny sky.
1 **L**ingering² onward dreamily.
In an **evening** of July.

Children three that sit down near,
2 **E**ager eye and willing ear,
Pleased a **simple** tale to hear.

Long has gone that sunny sky.
3 **E**choes³ **fade** and memories die.
Autumn⁴ cold has killed July.

Still she haunts⁵ me, phantomwise.
4 **A**lice moving under skies,
Never seen by waking eyes.

Children yet, the tale to hear,
5 **E**ager eye and willing ear,
Lovingly **shall** sit down near.

In a Wonderland they lie.
6 **D**reaming as the days go by.
Dreaming as the summers die:

Ever floating down the stream.
7 **L**ingering in the **golden** gleam.⁶
Life, what is it but a dream?

¹ **beneath** = under
² If you **linger** somewhere, you stay there longer than you need to.
³ An **echo** is a sound caused by a noise coming back after hitting a hard surface.
⁴ **Autumn** is the season after summer. It is also called **fall**.
⁵ If something **haunts** you, you keep thinking about it over a long period.
⁶ If something **gleams**, light comes off it because it is shiny.

7B Through the Looking Glass   95

Reading Comprehension

A Circle the correct answer.

Sequence **1.** Which of the following happened last?

    a. Dodgson wrote *Alice's Adventures in Wonderland*.
    b. Dodgson went in a rowboat with friends.
    c. *Through the Looking Glass* was published.

Paraphrase **2.** In lines 9–10, what does Dodgson mean by "almost as clearly as if it were yesterday."

    a. I remember it well.
    b. It only happened a short time ago.
    c. I wrote it down at the time.

Detail **3.** In each stanza (paragraph) of the poem, which lines rhyme with each other?

    a. the first and second   **b.** the first and last   **c.** all three

Vocabulary **4.** In stanza 5 of the poem, **shall** can be replaced by _____.

    a. should   **b.** call to   **c.** will

B **Strategy: Identifying the meaning of a poem.** Write the number of each stanza of the poem next to its meaning.

    a. _____ Alice and her sisters were excited to hear Dodgson's stories.

    b. _____ In day dreams, Dodgson remembers the day when he first told the story.

    c. _____ It has been a long time since the day the poem was written.

    d. _____ Different children, in the future, will want to hear the story.

    e. _____ The children will always be remembered through the story Dodgson created.

    f. _____ This is a description of the scene when the story was first told.

    g. _____ This is a reminder of the way the first Alice ends, with the character wondering if it was all a dream or if it was real.

Language Practice

A Vocabulary: Words in context. Answer the questions below. Share your answers with a partner.

1. Name three things that can **fade** over time.

2. Do you think you have a good **memory**?

3. What do you enjoy doing in the **evening**?

4. What is something you have never done, but are **eager** to try?

5. Look at a book you have. Which company **published** it?

6. What is some recent news that you were **pleased** to hear?

7. What are some examples of things that are **golden** in color?

8. Are you good at explaining difficult ideas using **simple** words?

B Grammar: Rhyming. In poetry, authors often use words that rhyme. Read these lines from the poem.

> Children three that sit down **near**,
> 2 Eager eye and willing **ear**,
> Pleased a simple tale to **hear**.
>
> Long has gone that sunny **sky**.
> 3 Echoes fade and memories **die**.
> Autumn cold has killed **July**.

Write a short poem, using rhyming words. Then read it to a partner.

_____

_____

_____

_____

_____

_____

Word Partners

Use *fade* with:
(adv.) fade **quickly**
(n.) **colors** fade, **images** fade,
memories fade
(v.) **begin to** fade

Lewis Carroll's Oxford

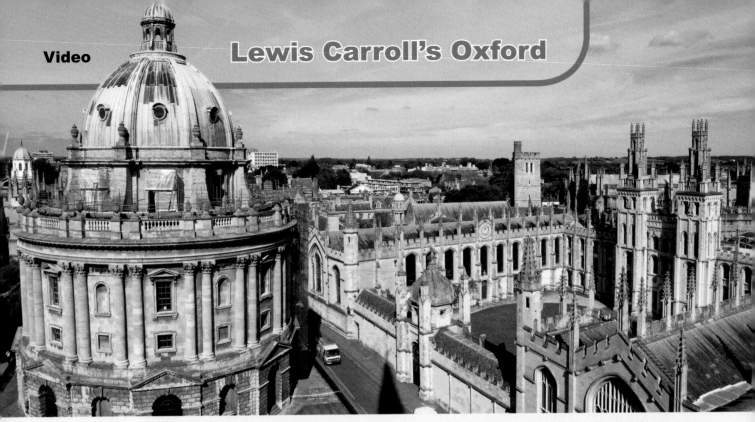

▲ Oxford University

A Preview. Many famous fantasy writers come from Oxford. Circle the writers you know, then try to match each to one of his or her books. With a partner, talk about the stories that you know.

1. Charles Lutwidge Dodgson   ○   ○ **a.** *Howl's Moving Castle*

2. J.R.R. Tolkien   ○   ○ **b.** *The Chronicles of Narnia*

3. C.S. Lewis   ○   ○ **c.** *Through the Looking Glass*

4. Diana Wynne Jones   ○   ○ **d.** *The Lord of the Rings*

B After you watch. Circle the correct answer in each sentence.

1. Oxford was named after (**a place where farmers crossed the river** / **the University there**).

2. People have been studying at the University of Oxford for over (**900** / **2,000**) years.

3. The Great Hall in Christ Church is famous because (**a movie was filmed there** / **many writers met there**).

4. The sheep in Dodgson's story was based on a real-life (**sheep** / **shopkeeper**).

5. The Inklings were (**a series of famous books** / **a group of writers**).

C Think about it. What, in particular, might inspire so many authors in Oxford?

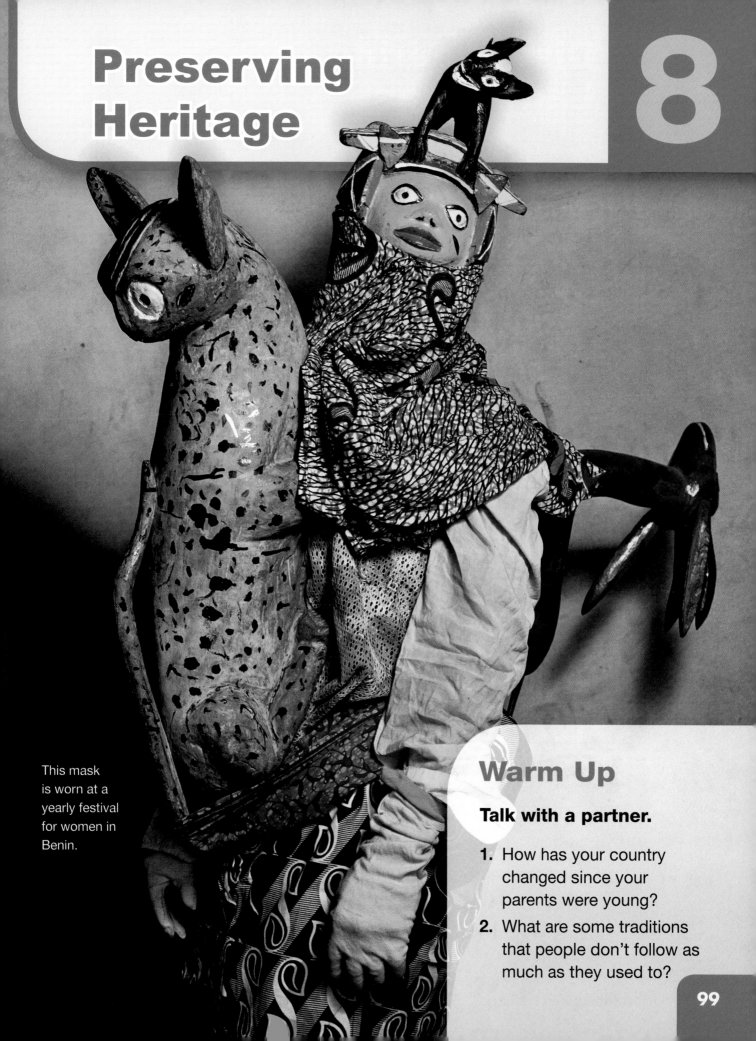

Preserving Heritage

This mask is worn at a yearly festival for women in Benin.

Warm Up

Talk with a partner.

1. How has your country changed since your parents were young?

2. What are some traditions that people don't follow as much as they used to?

Disappearing Languages

CENTRAL
SIBERIA

EASTERN
SIBERIA

Queen
Charlotte
Islands,
Canada

NORTHWEST
PACIFIC PLATEAU

CENTRAL
SOUTH AMERICA

NORTHERN
AUSTRALIA

More than half of the world's 7,000 languages may be extinct (no longer in use) by the year 2100. These are the top five areas in the world where languages are dying the fastest.

Before You Read

A Discussion. Look at the map above. Do you live near any of the areas where languages are dying? What kinds of people do you think speak these languages? Talk about your ideas with a partner.

B Definitions. Match the words with their meanings.

1. allow	**2.** amount	**3.** economic	**4.** express (*v.*)
5. local	**6.** reflect	**7.** respond	**8.** specific

_____ **a.** to show what you think or feel

_____ **b.** to let something happen

_____ **c.** to think carefully about something

_____ **d.** referring to a particular thing

_____ **e.** how much of something there is

_____ **f.** to reply

_____ **g.** about or related to a particular area

_____ **h.** related to the money and businesses of a country or society

Reading

Strategy: Predicting. What are some reasons why a language becomes endangered? Discuss with a partner. Read the passage to check your predictions.

Language Death

▲ Abamu Degio speaks Koro, an Indian language with about 800 native speakers. Linguists first learned about it in 2008.

1   Every 14 days, another language dies. There are many reasons for this. Some people think more common languages have more **economic** power. Because of this, young people choose to learn a common language as they think it is more useful. Another

5   reason is that some languages aren't written down. Guujaaw is a leader of the Haida Nation. His people have lived on the Queen Charlotte Islands, Canada, for more than 10,000 years. Their language is endangered.[1] Traditionally, it wasn't written down, and, as a result, some people are worried that it will die one day. Guujaaw **responds** to this, "We talk to each other, listen, visit, and **trust** the spoken word.

10   **Expressing** yourself without writing is natural." However, if Guujaaw's language and others like it are going to survive, writing may have to become part of their lives.

Too Important to Lose

    When a language dies, an amazing **amount** of knowledge dies with it. To begin with, language is a huge part of the culture of the people who speak

15   it. Language **allows** speakers to say **specific** things: words that describe a cultural idea may not translate exactly into another language. Furthermore, many endangered languages have rich spoken cultures. Stories, songs, and histories are passed on from older people to younger generations. Anthropologist Elizabeth Lindsey emphasizes this. "When an elder[2] dies,

20   a library is burned," she claims.

▲ Guujaaw, leader of the Haida Nation

    Language death also affects our knowledge about nature. Native tribes often have a deep understanding of **local** plants, animals, and ecosystems.[3] David Harrison, an expert on endangered languages, **reflects**. "Eighty percent of [plant and animal] species have been undiscovered by science. But that doesn't mean they're unknown to humans."

25 ## Still Hope

    Many languages are endangered. However, it's not too late. Children often grow up speaking two languages. "No one . . . becomes richer by abandoning[4] . . . one language to learn another," Harrison said. If children feel both languages are important, they will use both. Therefore, it is necessary that children realize how useful their local language is.

[1] A language that is **endangered** is one that is at risk of falling out of use.
[2] In some societies, an **elder** is one of the respected older people who have influence or power.
[3] An **ecosystem** includes all the plants and animals in an environment, and the relationship between them.
[4] When you **abandon** something, you stop using it.

Reading Comprehension

A Circle the correct answer.

Vocabulary 1. In line 9, the word **trust** means _____.

  a. remember   **b.** believe in   **c.** expect to

Paraphrase 2. What does the sentence "When an elder dies, a library is burned" (line 19) mean?

  a. When an elder dies, the people in the tribe start to forget them.
  b. When old people who speak an endangered language die, lots of knowledge dies too.
  c. People in some areas burn books when the leader of their tribe dies.

Detail 3. Harrison believes that _____ know about undiscovered animal species.

  a. scientists   **b.** language experts   **c.** local tribes

Inference 4. According to the passage, who is most important in stopping language death?

  a. elders   **b.** children   **c.** linguists

B **Strategy: Identifying fact and opinion.** Complete the statements below using one or two words from the passage. Then decide if each statement is a fact (**F**) or an opinion (**O**).

_____ 1. Languages die because they don't have as much _____ as other languages.

_____ 2. Endangered languages often aren't _____.

_____ 3. More common languages are more _____ for children to learn.

_____ 4. When languages die, we also lose _____ and histories of a group of people.

_____ 5. When we lose a language, we lose words that express _____ ideas.

_____ 6. If languages die, we lose knowledge about _____ and ecosystems.

A Quechua high ▶
school student in a
language class, Peru.

Language Practice

A Vocabulary: Words in context. Answer the questions below. Share your answers with a partner.

1. Name three countries with a powerful **economy**.

2. What was the last question you didn't know how to **respond** to?

3. Do you prefer to **express** yourself in writing or by speaking?

4. How many hours a night do you think is the right **amount** of sleep?

5. What do you wish your teacher would **allow** you to do in class?

6. What are two **specific** things you want to do this year?

7. What **local** foods should visitors to your city try? Why?

8. Do you usually make decisions quickly, or do you **reflect** for a while first?

B Grammar: Using *furthermore*. Read the example sentences. Sentence **a** is from the passage.

> **a.** Words that describe a cultural idea may not translate exactly into another language. **Furthermore**, many endangered languages have rich spoken cultures.
>
> **b.** To begin with, language is a huge part of the culture of the people who speak it. **Furthermore**, language allows speakers to say specific things.

Complete the first sentence using **furthermore**. Then write three more sentences. Read your sentences with a partner.

1. I don't like _____. Furthermore _____.

2. _____.

3. _____.

4. _____.

Word Partners

Use *local* with:
(n.) local **area**, local **artist**, local **business**, local **news**, local **office**, local **government**, local **police**

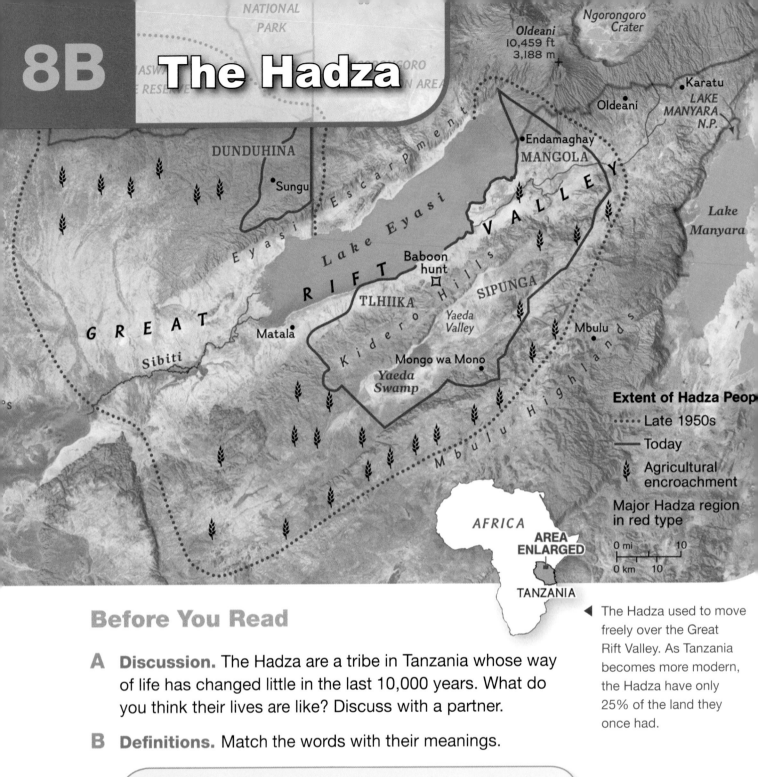

Ngorongoro
Crater

Oldeani
10,459 ft
3,188 m

Karatu
LAKE
MANYARA
N.P.

Oldeani

NATIONAL
PARK

DUNDUHINA

Sungu

Endamaghay
MANGOLA

Lake
Manyara

Eyasi Escarpment

Lake Eyasi

V A L L E Y

R I F T

Baboon
hunt

TLHIIKA

Kidero Hills

SIPUNGA

Yaeda
Valley

Mbulu

G R E A T

Matala

Mongo wa Mono

Sibiti

Yaeda
Swamp

Mbulu Highlands

Extent of Hadza Peop

····· Late 1950s

—— Today

Agricultural
encroachment

Major Hadza region
in red type

AFRICA

AREA
ENLARGED

0 mi   10

0 km   10

TANZANIA

◀ The Hadza used to move
freely over the Great
Rift Valley. As Tanzania
becomes more modern,
the Hadza have only
25% of the land they
once had.

Before You Read

A **Discussion.** The Hadza are a tribe in Tanzania whose way
of life has changed little in the last 10,000 years. What do
you think their lives are like? Discuss with a partner.

B **Definitions.** Match the words with their meanings.

> **1.** aware   **2.** fear   **3.** forget   **4.** freedom
> **5.** hurry   **6.** medical   **7.** opportunity   **8.** raise

_____ **a.** to move or do something quickly   _____ **e.** knowing about something

_____ **b.** the condition of being able to do   _____ **f.** to keep animals or grow
　　　　 whatever you want　　　　　　　　　　　　　　　 plants on a farm

_____ **c.** to not remember   _____ **g.** the feeling of being scared

_____ **d.** related to helping sick people   _____ **h.** a chance to do something

Reading

△ Hadza women dance in celebration.

Strategy: Scanning. The Hadza own very few things. What are some of the things they own? _____

What have we forgotten?

1   They grow no food and **raise** no livestock. They live without calendars. In fact, they don't count hours, days, or months. The Hadza language doesn't even have words for numbers past three or four. Consequently, they don't celebrate birthdays or anniversaries. Their way of life has changed very little for the last 10,000 years.

△ Hadza men follow an animal's trail.

5   To the outside world, this way of living may be hard to understand. We may think that there's nothing the Hadza can teach us. Michael Finkel, a journalist,[1] would disagree. He had the **opportunity** to spend two weeks with the Hadza and said that being with them changed the way he looked at the world.

So what can we learn from the Hadza? One thing is their attitude toward life. Each Hadza tribesperson owns very little: a cooking pot, a water container, an ax, and a bow. The things they own can be wrapped[2]
10   in a blanket and carried. This teaches us that perhaps modern city-living people don't really need everything they own.

We can also learn about their **freedom** from stress. Their lives are incredibly dangerous, and **medical** help is far away. One bad fall from a tree, or one bite from a poisonous snake can leave a member of the Hadza dead. Yet they don't worry about the future—or anything. Finkel described the change in his
15   feelings as "the Hadza effect." He said that after being with the Hadza, he felt calmer.[3] He wasn't in such a **hurry**, and was more **aware** of the present. He also felt more self-sufficient[4] and had less **fear**. "My time with the Hadza made me happier," he said.

[1] A **journalist** is a person whose job is to write for newspapers, magazines, TV, etc.
[2] When you **wrap** something, you fold something around it.
[3] When you are **calm**, you don't show or feel any worry, anger, or excitement.
[4] Someone who is **self-sufficient** doesn't need to depend on other people.

Reading Comprehension

A Circle the correct answer.

Detail **1.** The Hadza don't celebrate yearly events because they don't _____ like we do.

    a. like celebrating   **b.** remember things   **c.** count time

Detail **2.** After spending time with the Hadza, Finkel changed _____.

    a. the way he spent his free time

    b. his ideas about the world

    c. the clothes and shoes he wore

Inference **3.** The Hadza probably _____ food.

    a. buy   **b.** hunt for   **c.** raise animals for

Detail **4.** Which of these is NOT part of *the Hadza effect* (line 15)?

    a. better health   **b.** a relaxed attitude   **c.** a slower way of life

B **Strategy: Classification.** Which group of people do these things match? Write **a** to **f** in the correct place on the chart.

    a. Owning a lot of things is not very important.

    b. Life is sometimes dangerous.

    c. They worry about what will happen a few years from now.

    d. They celebrate birthdays.

    e. They live almost the same way as some people did thousands of years ago.

    f. Their food comes from farms.

people in cities

the Hadza

both

Language Practice

A **Vocabulary: Words in context.** In each sentence, circle the best answer. The words in **blue** are from the reading.

1. Which of these is easier to **forget**?
   a. a long number   **b.** your name

2. Some people **raise** _____.
   a. goats   **b.** bicycles

3. If you take an **opportunity**, you _____ something.
   a. do   **b.** miss

4. To be able to _____ is an example of **freedom**.
   a. speak English well   **b.** say what you want

5. **Medical** help includes _____.
   a. X-rays   **b.** teaching

6. When you are **in a hurry**, you _____ time.
   a. have a lot of   **b.** don't have much

7. Which of these are you more likely to be **aware** of?
   a. a noise near you   **b.** a secret

8. Most people _____ the feeling of **fear**.
   a. enjoy   **b.** dislike

> ## Usage
>
> *raise* and *rise*
> *Raise* also means "to move something to a higher position." E.g. *Students raise their hands when they want to speak in class.*
> *Rise* means that something moves upward: *Smoke rises from a fire.*

B **Grammar: Using *consequently*.** Read the example sentences. Sentence **a** is from the passage.

> **a.** The Hadza language doesn't even have words for numbers past three or four. **Consequently**, they don't celebrate birthdays or anniversaries.
>
> **b.** The bugs look like thorns. **Consequently**, animals stay away from them.
>
> **c.** Scientists thought animals couldn't live without the sun's energy. **Consequently**, scientists never expected to find living creatures down there.

Complete the sentences. Then read them with a partner.

1. More schools teach English. Consequently, _____.

2. More people are aware of language death. Consequently, _____

_____.

3. _____.

Video
Saving Languages

Aboriginal artist
Turkey Tolson Tjupurrula,
Central Desert, Australia

A Preview. The video discusses the languages of Aboriginal people in Australia. What do you know about Australian Aborigines? Talk about your ideas with a partner.

B After you watch. Circle the correct answers.

1. Aborigines have lived in the area of the Northern Territory for (**about 5,000** / **more than 50,000**) years.

2. Greg Anderson and David Harrison are members of the (**Enduring Voices** / **Lost Languages**) Project.

3. The project calls an area with a large number of endangered languages a "language (**focus area** / **hotspot**)."

4. The team uses old (**photos** / **maps**) to find out where languages were spoken in the past.

5. The team meets Charlie, (**an important local linguist** / **the last living speaker of Amurdag**).

6. Greg and David watch a teacher of Yawuru, a language with (**no** / **very few**) native speakers today.

C Think about it. Why do you think the attitudes toward local languages in Australia are changing?

Vocabulary Review

Complete the sentences below using the words in parentheses.
One word in each sentence is extra.

1. My sister always _____ that the _____ on that TV show are _____.
   So, she was really _____ when she heard that an actor she likes had been
   _____ the main _____. (**boring**, **characters**, **complains**, **economic**,
   offered, **pleased**, **role**)

2. The sunlight turned from a bright _____ color to a deep red, and the light began to
   _____. The hikers realized that they had only minutes before the _____ came,
   and they had to _____ to reach their camp before dark. (**aware**, **evening**, **fade**,
   golden, **hurry**)

3. Medical students need to have good _____ because there is a huge _____ of
   information they must not _____. (**amount**, **forget**, **memories**, **respond**)

4. In the _____ news section of our newspaper this morning, they _____ an
   article about a woman who lives on my street. (**in particular**, **local**, **published**)

World Heritage Notes

Notes Completion. Scan the information
on pages 110 and 111 to complete the notes.

What: Saryarka

Where: Kazakhstan

Data:

• Saryarka was the first World Heritage Site in _____.

• The endangered _____ – a kind of antelope – lives here.

• The wetlands provide _____ and _____
  to many species of migrating birds, like the Siberian white crane and
  _____.

• This is one of the main sites in Kazakhstan for _____.

• The people who live on the steppe are called the _____.

• They have a tradition of using _____ to help them hunt.

Saryarka

Site: **Saryarka—Steppe and Lakes of Northern Kazakhstan**

Location: **The Kostanay and Akmola Provinces, Kazakhstan**

Category: **Natural**

Status: **World Heritage Site since 2008**

Kazakhstan

Stretching over about 4,500 square kilometers of Kazakhstan, Saryarka World Heritage Site was the first World Heritage Site in Central Asia.

The site includes two large reserves, which together protect and preserve large areas of the Kazakh steppe.

The reserves also protect other environments, such as ancient pine forests and lakes. This variety of landscapes provides homes to many animals, such as marmots, wolves, and the saiga, a kind of antelope.

The site also protects the region's wetlands, an important area which provides food and rest for many species of migrating birds. Every year more than fifteen million birds—including many endangered species—stop here on the way to western and eastern Siberia. Birds like the extremely rare Siberian white crane and pink flamingos come here to find food, and spend the winter. This has made the site one of the most popular areas in Kazakhstan for bird-watching.

Despite its beauty, the steppe is a difficult place to live. The weather on the steppe can be very extreme. It can sometimes be very hot, and sometimes very cold. However, groups of people have lived in this rough environment for centuries. They are known as the Kazakhs. Today, some of these tribes still live and work on the steppe, moving their families and homes all over the area to find food for their animals. One tradition that has helped the Kazakhs survive in this environment is the art of hunting with eagles. The eagle hunters and their highly-trained golden eagles are an important part of life on the steppe. Once they have trained to hunt together, each man and his eagle are lifelong partners, and help to keep the Kazakhs' traditions and culture alive.

Review 4

A KAZAKH FOLKTALE
ALDAR KOSE AND THE MAGIC COAT

1 One winter's day, Aldar Kose was riding through the steppe. It was very cold, and he had only an old, torn coat to wear. He tried to ride faster, but his old horse would not move any faster.

Suddenly, he saw a rider on a beautiful horse coming quickly toward him. The
5 rider was wearing a warm, thick coat. Soon, Aldar Kose recognized him as a local rich man. This man was very greedy and selfish. Aldar Kose soon thought up a cunning plan.

He moved his hat to the side of his head and opened his torn coat. Then, he sat up straight, and started singing a happy song, acting as if he wasn't cold at all.

10 The rich man was surprised Aldar Kose was acting this way. He rode up, and asked, "Are you really not cold?"

"Your coat may be warm, but mine is making me hot," replied Aldar Kose.

"How can your coat make you hot?" said the rich man, "It is so thin, and there are holes in it!"

15 "It is a magic coat," said Aldar Kose. "The holes let out the cold, and the warmth stays with me." Aldar Kose looked so comfortable the man believed him. At once, the greedy man wanted the "magic coat" for himself. He wanted to buy it, but Aldar Kose refused.

"I will give you my coat in exchange! It is very warm." said the rich man.

20 Aldar Kose still refused. "But, if you give me your horse too, I will think about it," he said.

The rich man agreed. Aldar Kose took off his old coat and came down from his horse. He put on the warm, thick coat, got onto the rich man's horse, and quickly rode off across the steppe.

Reading Comprehension

Identifying cause and effect. Match the causes and effects to make sentences.

1. Aldar Kose's coat was old and torn   o   o   **a.** so he wanted to buy it.

2. Aldar Kose acted as if he wasn't cold,   o   o   **b.** and got a new coat and horse.

3. Aldar Kose looked so comfortable that   o   o   **c.** the rich man believed him.

4. The rich man thought it was a magic coat,   o   o   **d.** so he was very cold in the winter.

5. Aldar Kose tricked the rich man   o   o   **e.** so the rich man thought his coat was magic.

Language Extension

A   Describing people. Match the words in the box with their definitions.

> comfortable   cunning   greedy   local   selfish

_____ **1.** belonging to the place where you live

_____ **2.** wanting more than is needed or fair

_____ **3.** having the ability to do things in a clever way

_____ **4.** relaxed and happy

_____ **5.** caring only about himself or herself

B   Fill in the blanks with the words from A.

1. The _____ girl wouldn't share her toys with the other children.

2. Don't be so _____! Take only what you can eat.

3. The thief was very _____, and managed steal the money.

4. I don't like going out. I am most _____ when I'm at home.

5. Our tour guide in Brazil was a _____ man. He had lived there his whole life.

1 Spider Webs

Narrator: There are spiders all around the world. Scientists think there are about 40,000 spider species on Earth. Many people find these small creatures very scary, and want to stay away from them, but others find the webs they make beautiful.

Webs are made from silky threads, from the spider's body. These threads of spider silk are 30 times thinner than human hair. If a single thread of this silk went all the way around the Earth it would weigh less than half a kilogram. It's the strongest kind of thread in nature, but it is amazingly light and very flexible.

This is an orb weaving spider. And this is a bat. The bat uses its hearing to help it to fly at night without hitting anything. Well . . . almost anything. This spider's web is huge and very sticky. Suddenly, the bat is trapped. And that is that.

The net casting spider uses a different kind of web. It doesn't make a web. Instead, it and its sticky silk hang from above, like a trap. Then it waits for its meal to walk by. Suddenly, the spider jumps and throws its silk out to catch the insect. Then, it folds the silk around the insect, so it can eat it later.

Different spiders make different kinds of silk. Each type of silk has a different use. Sometimes their webs are in the shape of long threads. These threads have a very sticky liquid all over them. When an insect touches the thread, the liquid covers it, and it stops the insect from getting away.

A spider knows exactly what is happening at the center of its web. It keeps one foot on a thread that goes all the way to the center. When an insect moves on the web, the spider can sense the movements. It realizes its dinner has arrived. When the spider isn't hungry, it keeps the insect in silk, to eat later.

It is the combination of strength and flexibility in a spider's silk that has provided it with its next meal.

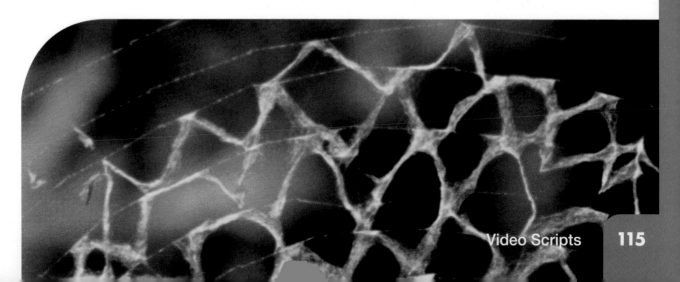

2 Bionic Eyes

Narrator: They may be considered the windows to our souls, but our eyes are built mainly to sense light, and translate it into electrical signals the brain can understand. It is these signals that form pictures of the world in our minds. That is how we see.

For the last ten years, Linda Morfoot has been completely blind. But now, a new technology is allowing her to once more see the world that surrounds her. Linda cannot see with her own eyes because in her eyes, the retina, a layer of light-sensitive cells lining the inner surface of the eye, has been damaged. Being blind can be very scary and confusing.

Linda Morfoot: It's frustrating to lose your sight because you run into things, you run into people. You trip over things. It's just frustrating.

Narrator: Now, thanks to Dr. Mark Humayun of the University of Southern California, she may see again.

Dr. Mark Humayun: All along, we've been told it's impossible. It's science fiction. It can't happen.

Narrator: Dr. Humayun and others in his industry are proving it is possible for someone like Linda to see once more.

To see, Linda has to wear a very special pair of glasses. There's a camera in the center of the glasses. That camera sends signals to a small computer. Through an operation, the doctors have put another tiny computer under Linda's skin. A very thin, flexible, wire comes out one end of this computer. At the end of the wire is a small metal disc. The doctors put this disc into Linda's eyes, touching the part of Linda's eyes that would usually sense light, the retina. The machine is controlled by light. When the camera senses light, the tiny computer imitates what a real eye would do. It turns the light into electrical signals that Linda's retina can sense.

Doctor: Do you see the light? → **Linda:** Yeah → **Doctor:** Is it bright?
Linda: Yeah. → **Doctor:** Very bright? → **Linda:** Yeah.

Narrator: The retina then sends the messages to Linda's brain. With these machines, Linda is beginning to see again.

Linda: One. Two. Three. Four. That's all.

Narrator: So now after 10 years of blindness, Linda can see the grandchildren she hasn't seen before.

In time, the doctors think Linda will be able to combine more information with the little bits that she can see, to help her live a full and independent life.

3 The Lost City

Narrator: Life as we know it. Scientists used to think that all life on Earth needed light to survive. But then, scientists discovered that life exists here, too. In the deep, dark, ocean, far below the surface of the sea.

First they found animals living near underwater volcanoes called black smokers. Now they've discovered life in an even more extraordinary place.

They call it "Lost City."

The Lost City is in the North-Atlantic Ocean, in a huge group of undersea mountains.

These scientists are preparing a robot, called Hercules, to explore Lost City. National Geographic explorer Bob Ballard says exploring Lost City is like going into outer space.

Bob Ballard: What is amazing to me is that we didn't go into the largest feature on Earth until after Neil Armstrong and Buzz Aldrin went to the moon. In fact, now we have better maps of Mars than we have of the deep sea beneath the waves. It's amazing.

Narrator: Here the sea water is extremely hot. But, somehow, many creatures seem to thrive here. The scientists didn't expect to find any animals here. It's 200 degrees Celsius, hotter than boiling water. And the water is filled with chemicals that can kill life.

The scientists use robots that they can control from the surface. These robots collect and bring up creatures that live in Lost City, so the scientists can study them. They believe these animals may survive here because there are a lot of tiny creatures, called microbes, for them to eat.

The existence of places like this on Earth make Ballard and other scientists wonder. Could places like Lost City exist on other planets? Ballard thinks it's possible.

Bob Ballard: What we're discovering is that, uh, life is much more creative than we ever thought it was. And there will be many other expeditions not only on our planet, looking for exotic life forms living in extreme environments, but in outer space itself.

Narrator: Meanwhile, scientists will continue to study Lost City— trying to discover what other secrets it can tell us about life . . . how it started— and where we can find it.

4 | Survival: Building a Fire

Narrator: Fire. For more than a million years, it has provided humans with warmth, light, and protection. But it's easy to forget how useful fire is, until you don't have it. Consider this: What if you were lost in the desert or jungle? Could you start a fire?

This is a bow drill. It is a simple, ancient tool used to start fires. Today, Boyd Matson is learning to start a fire. But as Boyd soon realizes, the process of starting a fire is not easy. He needs someone to teach him how to do it. Tim McWelch and Rick Hugh Houston are survival guides.

Boyd: Where there's smoke, hopefully there will soon be fire. These are the guys I've been looking for, Tim and Hugh. Can you teach a novice how to do this?

Survival Guide: Absolutely. It just takes some time, a little bit of practice, and the right materials.

Narrator: To make the drill and the board that goes under it, they need to find wood that is not too soft or too hard.

Survival Guide: Okay, this is a sycamore tree, and this is a medium hardwood. We can use this as wood for drills and boards.

Narrator: They also need some dry wood to use as fuel. Next, Tim teaches Boyd how to use the drill. The string tied to the bow drill needs to be really tight. And in less than 10 minutes, they have made fire.

Well, sort of.

That's just the first part of Boyd's lesson. Now he has to prove that he can do it on his own. The experts only provide Boyd with two things—a knife, and a piece of string. Everything else has to come from the forest. He has one hour to make a fire.

Once Boyd has enough wood, he begins to build his fireboard, and his drill. He ties the string to a long piece of wood, and bends it to make his bow. Now he needs to put together other types of wood, as fuel for his fire.

Boyd: I've got my firebox that I've made with my little hole in it, my drill, my block that goes on top of the drill, my bow. Now all I've got to do is make fire.

So frustrating. Arrgghhh!

Narrator: Turning the drill makes the wood hot. When the wood is very hot, Boyd must blow on it, to start the fire. Making a fire is hard work. And it takes Boyd a long time. Not one, not two, but almost 3 hours. It's about to go out. Boyd blows on the dry wood some more. Finally, there's smoke coming from the wood, Boyd's managed to start a fire.

Survival Guide: Well done, sir.

Boyd: Thank you, guys.

Survival Guide: Congratulations.

Narrator: Boyd may not have achieved his goal of starting a fire in an hour. But he has learned an important new skill that may help him stay alive in a survival situation.

5 Race to the Moon

President Kennedy: We choose to go to the moon in this decade.

Narrator: Less than seven years after President Kennedy said those words, people around the world saw one of the greatest moments of their generation—the moment humans first walked on the moon. The story of the first trip to the moon is a tale of new ideas, of hope, and of courage.

It's also a story about two countries, the U.S. and the Soviet Union.

President John F. Kennedy made his first speech about sending a man to the moon in May 1961. At that time, the Soviet Union had already started to explore the space beyond our planet. In October 1957, the Soviet Union launched Sputnik, the world's first satellite, into space. Then, the Soviets became the first nation to send a person into space. This was a major win for them.

But the American space program was not far behind. In 1961, the first American astronaut, Alan Shepard, went into space. Then in 1963, U.S. astronaut John Glenn went around the Earth a total of three times. Over the next eight years, in the Apollo program, NASA prepared to send three astronauts to the moon.

They made great discoveries about space, and, finally, on July 20, 1969, Apollo 11 landed two people safely on the surface of the moon. The images they sent back amazed the whole world.

Neil Armstrong: That's one small step for man, one giant leap for mankind.

In the decades since 1969, the American space program has had many more successes. Today, NASA continues to investigate our universe, and it continues to develop new technologies, and the equipment to do it. Just like it did in the 1960s during the early days of the Space Race.

However, instead of competing with each other, Russian and American astronauts, like this crew on the International Space Station, can now be found working together to expand our knowledge about what's beyond our planet.

6 Where Writing Began

Narrator: Over 9,000 years ago, in the deserts of what is now Iraq, the civilizations of Mesopotamia developed between the Tigris and Euphrates rivers. From the ruins of their cities and the writings they left behind, we know, the people of this ancient land were called the Sumerians.

Around 5,000 B.C., they began to grow their own food, and keep animals. In order to exist in the desert, they learned to control the surrounding environment. They developed ways to store the flood waters that flowed for a short time each year.

As their population increased, the Sumerians built cities like Ur and Nineveh. The remains of these cities still exist today. Within each city was a huge temple. It had places to keep food, to keep treasure, as well as houses for the city officials and, of course, places for worship.

As society became more complex, the Sumerians realized they needed some way to record information. Thus, it is here that writing was invented. Early forms of writing were very simple. They pressed sharp pieces of wood into pieces of wet clay, to make pictures. Called *cuneiform*, these characters represented objects and numbers and made up the first written language.

They also used it to write down the first major written story, the legend of King Gilgamesh, the king who wanted to live forever.

Perhaps the best known of Mesopotamia's civilizations was Babylon, the center of a kingdom that went across southern Iraq and beyond. Its hanging gardens were considered a wonder of the ancient world, and its king, Hammurabi, published a set of laws that was quite similar to many of the laws we have today.

Much of Sumerian culture has faded from memory, but researchers investigating these ruins are learning more and more about these amazing people every day.

7 Lewis Carroll's Oxford

Narrator: About 80 kilometers north-west of London is the city of Oxford. Oxford began as "Ford of the Oxen," a simple place for farmers to take their cattle across the river. Today it is a city, famous for being the home of the University of Oxford, the oldest university in the English-speaking world.

Although no one knows exactly when the university began, historians know that people were teaching and studying here as far back as 1096. Today, more than 900 years later, it is a combination of the university's fame and the beauty of its buildings that brings thousands of visitors here each year.

One of the largest colleges in Oxford is Christ Church College. In recent years, the college building, in particular, its Great Hall, has become famous as a filming location for the Harry Potter movies.

But Christ Church is also well known as the home of Charles Lutwidge Dodgson, also known as Lewis Carroll. And it was at Christ Church that Dodgson first met the children of the head of the College, Henry Liddell. The Liddell children, in particular, young Alice Pleasance Liddell, became good friends with Dodgson.

He took them on boat rides along the river, and told them many stories. One of these stories told the adventures of a girl called Alice in a confusing underground land that he called Wonderland. Although the stories were fantastic and strange, Dodgson based them on situations, places, and people that were familiar to the children.

For example: in *Through the Looking Glass*, Alice visits a shop where she meets a sheep, and things on the shelves float away when Alice tries to look at them. Many believe the shop in the story represents a small shop just across the road from Christ Church. In Dodgson's time, the shopkeeper was an old woman with a sheep-like voice. The shop itself was often flooded with water from a nearby stream.

However, it is not unusual for Oxford to appear in fantasy stories. Besides Dodgson, the city has also influenced the writing of other great fantasy writers, like Philip Pullman and Diana Wynne Jones, and most famously, J.R.R. Tolkien, and C.S. Lewis. These two writers formed a writing club called the Inklings. They often met here, at the Eagle and the Child. And it was here that Lewis' Narnia series, and Tolkien's Lord of the Rings began to take shape.

Having inspired so many wonderful writers and their amazing stories, it is no wonder the city of Oxford will be visited and treasured for a long time to come.

8 Saving Languages

Narrator: Australia's Northern Territory. Australia's native people, the Aborigines, have lived in this area for more than 50,000 years.

A group of researchers from the Enduring Voices project has come here to find and study the local languages, many of which are in danger of becoming extinct. The team's mission is to visit language hotspots, areas around the world where there are a high number of languages that are endangered. The situation in Australia is bad. Over a hundred native languages are endangered.

The researchers' guide teaches them about how the Aboriginal people lived—and how these cultures survived in the desert. Many cultures do not write these things down, and, consequently, once the language stops being spoken the knowledge is lost.

The team studies old maps and writings, and works with local researchers, to find out where specific languages were spoken in the past. Then, they look for people who might still speak the language.

On this trip, they get an opportunity to meet a man named Charlie. Charlie is the last person on Earth who speaks a language called Amurdag. But he doesn't remember many Amurdag words because he hasn't used the language since he was young. The team takes Charlie to a place that was special to his ancestors. Here, Charlie manages to remember a few simple Amurdag words. He tells the team what each word means.

Researcher: Iraba.

Charlie: Iraba ayoowa.

Researcher: That's my father . . .

Charlie: Arabai my father.

Researcher: How would you say my mother?

Charlie: Aowano . . . my mother . . .

Narrator: The team is eager to hear every word Charlie can remember. And they record every moment of their time with him.

The team is also working to make people more aware of the problem. Their goal is to use cameras and modern sound equipment to help these "last speakers" record as much of their language as possible.

In Australia, this means teaching a new generation an old language. There are many reasons the children of today didn't learn their grandparents' languages. These children are learning Yawuru, which has only three speakers left. The children and their teachers hope they will become fluent Yawuru speakers.

With so many languages in danger, these researchers, and many others, must hurry to save all they can.

Indexes

Target Vocabulary Index

Reading Strategy Index

Grammar Index

Photo Credits

1 Beverly Joubert/NGIC, **3** Wikipedia.org/Public Domain, **4** (tl to b) Chris Rainier/NGIC, Emory Kristof/NGIC, Mark Thiessen/NGIC, John F. Kennedy Presidential Library and Museum/Public Domain, alle/Shutterstock, **5** (tl to b) Chris Hill/NGIC, Lynn Abercrombie/NGIC, Chris Rainier/NGIC, Martin Schoeller/NGIC, Frans Lanting/NGIC, **6, 7** (t, l to r) Carrie Vonderhaar/Ocean Futures Society/NGIC, Todd Gipstein/NGIC, alle/Shutterstock, Stuart Franklin/NGIC, William H. Bond/NGIC, NASA Images/Public Domain, Wikipedia.org/Public Domain, O.V.D./Shutterstock, Space/NASA Sites/Public Domain, John Burcham/NGIC, Mark Thiessen/NGIC, Joel Sartore/NGIC, Phyllis Galembo/NGIC, Frans Lanting/NGIC, Chris Hill/NGIC, **11** Carrie Vonderhaar/Ocean Futures Society/NGIC, **12** Christian Ziegler/NGIC, **13** (t to b) Christian Ziegler/NGIC, Pete Oxford/Minden Pictures, alle/Shutterstock, **16** Darlyne A. Murawski/NGIC, **17** (t to b) Darlyne A. Murawski/NGIC, Doug Stern/NGIC, **18** Michael Melford/NGIC, **20** Amy White & Al Petteway/NGIC, **21** Mark Thiessen/NGIC, **22** Mark Thiessen/NGIC, **23** (t to b) Mark Thiessen/NGIC, **26** Max Aguilera-Hellweg/NGIC, **27** (t to b) Max Aguilera-Hellweg/NGIC, **28** Max Aguilera-Hellweg/NGIC, **31** Stuart Franklin/NGIC, (b) Greg801/iStockphoto, **32–33** Stuart Franklin/NGIC, **33** (t to b) Frans Lanting/NGIC, Tui De Roy/Minden Pictures/NGIC, Mark Moffett/Minden Pictures/NGIC, **37** Frans Lanting/NGIC, **38–39** (all) Frans Lanting/NGIC, **42** Emory Kristof/NGIC, **43** Emory Kristof/NGIC, **46** Stephen Low Distribution Inc., **47** John Burcham/NGIC, **48** Joel Sartore/NGIC, **49** (t to b) IMAGNO/Viktor Frankl Archive, Yossi Ghinsberg, **52** Daily Mail/Rex/Alamy, **53** Royal Navy/PPL Ltd, **56** (t to b) Michael Melford/NGIC, Sjoerd van der Wal/iStockphoto, **57** Chris Rainier/NGIC, (b) Greg801/iStockphoto, **58–59** Chris Rainier/NGIC, **63** Wikipedia.org/Public Domain, **64** NASA/JPL/Space Science Institute/NGIC, **65** NASA/JPL/Space Science Institute/NGIC, **66** NASA/JPL/Space Science Institute/NGIC, **68** NASA/Public Domain, **69** (t to b) John F. Kennedy Presidential Library and Museum/Public Domain, Wikipedia.org/Public Domain, Wikipedia.org/Public Domain, **72** (t to b) Nasa Images/Public Domain, Space/NASA Sites, **73** Todd Gipstein/NGIC, **78** Clifton R. Adams/NGIC, **79** Wikipedia.org/Public Domain, **82** Lynn Abercrombie/NGIC, **83** Chris Hill/NGIC, (b) Greg801/iStockphoto, **84–85** Chris Hill/NGIC, Pecold/Shutterstock, **89** Sam Abell/NGIC, **90** Sam Abell/NGIC, **91** Sam Abell/NGIC, **92** Publications Art/NGIC, **94** Sam Abell/NGIC, **95** (t to b) Sam Abell/NGIC, Annie Griffiths/NGIC, Fedorov Oleksiy/Shutterstock, **97** Fedorov Oleksiy/Shutterstock, **98** Andrei Nekrassov/Shutterstock, **99** Phyllis Galembo/NGIC, **101** (t to b) Chris Rainier/NGIC, Dewitt Jones/NGIC, **102** Michael S. Lewis/NGIC, **105** (all) Martin Schoeller/NGIC, **108** Frans Lanting/NGIC, **109** David Edwards/NGIC, (b) Greg801/iStockphoto, **110–111** David Edwards/NGIC, **115** Darlyne A. Murawski/NGIC, **119** Michael Melford/NGIC, **120–121** NASA/Public Domain, **124–125** Michael S. Lewis/NGIC

Illustration Credits

32, 58, 84, 100, 110 National Geographic Maps, **14** Page2 LLC, **18–19** Page2 LLC, **24** Bryan Christie Design/NGIC, **30** Bryan Christie Design/NGIC, **34–35** Eric Foenander, **36** Page2 LLC, **54** Bryan Christie Design/NGIC, **60–61** Eric Foenander, **70** Page2 LLC, **74–76** Page2 LLC, **80** Page2 LLC, **82** Bernard D'Andrea/NGIC, **86–87** Eric Foenander, **90** William H. Bond/NGIC, **96** Page2 LLC, **104** Martin Gamache/National Geographic, **106** Page2 LLC, **112–113** Eric Foenander

Text Credits

13 Adapted from "The Art of Deception," by Natalie Angier: NGM, August 2009, **17** Adapted from "Deadly Silk," by Richard Conniff: NGM, August 2001, **23** Adapted from "Bionics," by Josh Fischman: NGM, January 2010, **27** Adapted from "Robots," by Chris Carroll: NGM, August 2011, **35** Traditional tale, **39** Adapted from "Earth in the Beginning," by Tim Appenzeller and Frans Lanting: NGM, December 2006, **43** Adapted from "Deep Sea Vents," by Richard A. Lutz: NGM, October 2000, **49** Adapted from "Everyday Survival," by Laurence Gonzalez: http://adventure.nationalgeographic.com/2008/08/everyday-survival/laurence-gonzalez-text, **53** Adapted from "Left for Dead," by Nick Ward and Sinéad O'Brien: National Geographic Adventure, August 2007, **61** Traditional tale, **65** Adapted from "Beautiful Stranger," by Bill Douthitt: NGM, December 2006, **69** Adapted from "We Choose to Go to the Moon," by John F. Kennedy: Address at Rice University, 12 September 1962, **75** Adapted from "The Power of Writing," by Cary Wolinsky: NGM, August 1999, **79** Adapted from "The Companionship of Books," by Arthur Elmore Bostwick from "A Librarian's Open Shelf: Essays on Various Subjects," 1920, **87** Traditional tale, **91** Adapted from "The Wonderland of Lewis Carroll," by Cathy Newman: NGM, June 1991, **95** Adapted from "Through the Looking-Glass," by Lewis Carroll, 1871, **101** Adapted from "Disappearing Languages," by Enduring Voices Project: http://travel.nationalgeographic.com/travel/enduring-voices/, **105** Adapted from "The Hadza," by Michael Finkel: NGM, December 2009, **113** Traditional tale

National Geographic Image Collection = NGIC
National Geographic Magazine = NGM